THE PERFECT
PONY

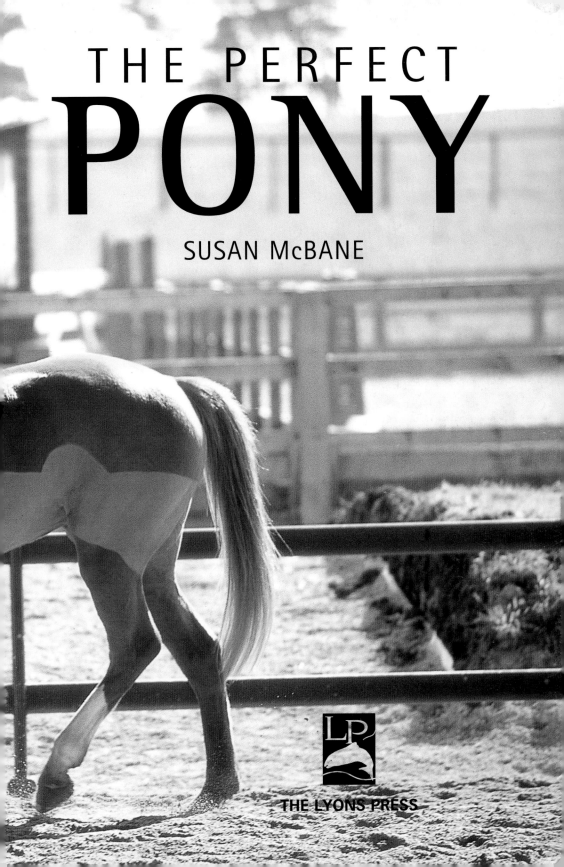

THE PERFECT
PONY

SUSAN McBANE

THE LYONS PRESS

Executive editor – **Julian Brown**
Assistant editor – **Sharon Ashman**
Creative art director – **Keith Martin**
Executive art editor – **Leigh Jones**
Book design – **Peter Gerrish**
Production – **Lee Sargent**

First Lyons Press edition, 2001

First published in Great Britain in 2001 by Hamlyn, an imprint of
Octopus Publishing Group Limited, 2–4 Heron Quays, London E14 4JP

Produced by Toppan Printing Company Ltd
Printed in China

10 9 8 7 6 5 4 3 2 1

contents

introduction

There seems to be no end to the popularity of ponies and riding. As we humans become more and more stressed by our modern environment and lives, ponies, and other animals, seem to open the way to a more natural life, to relationships with other beings who provide a completely different world into which we can escape and find relief from our human problems.

Animals are a fascinating blend of similarities to ourselves but differences from us, too. Although they, too, need food, water, fresh air, company and shelter and need to exercise, to take care of their health and to be allowed to be the type of animal they are and do the things their kind does – pony things, dog things, guinea pig things or whatever – their outlook on life is not at all the same as ours. Although wild-living equines such as asses, zebras and also feral horses and ponies are known to have migration patterns, moving around often many kilometres or miles to reach fresh, often traditional, grazing grounds, as far as their daily lives are concerned they do not seem to plan ahead for more than a few minutes. They truly live 'in the moment' and have an ability to concentrate on the here and now in a way we seem to find very difficult. When we take on the care of and the responsibility for an animal, we are actually placing ourselves under even more stress than we may have already! However, this stress has a definite upside: if we meet our obligations properly we receive so very much more in return that the chores seem insignificant in relation to our rewards.

Ponies are very special animals. They are unique in that no other animal has been so important and useful to mankind, not even the dog. No other animal is so strong that he can carry or pull our weight at great speed for many miles. No other animal has provided us, over the millenia, with food, transport, friendship, power, fun and fulfilment like the horse has. (When we say 'horse' we mean 'pony', of course, because horses and ponies are of the same biological species; just their sizes and characters are different.) Horses and ponies have made possible the building of empires and the winning of wars, the farming of land, the development of industries, have improved communication and travel and, in modern times, have provided us with a unique means of having fun. They have little idea of what competition means in our terms, but they enable us to cover ourselves with glory and win prizes and money, to indulge in a consuming hobby or to earn our livings.

In return for all this it is little to ask that we realize how unique and important ponies are and to accept the big responsibility of looking after them properly. They are not cheap animals to keep unless you have enough land of your own on which they can graze and live. Livery or boarding charges are quite high, particularly to those not on generous

Above right: *Ponies which are athletic and good performance ponies will cost more to buy and keep, as competing can be expensive.*

Right: *A good pony can be your companion and teacher.*

incomes, and veterinary fees, farriers' bills and the purchase of tack, harness and equipment are all expensive but have to be budgeted for. Travelling to events, entering competitions and registering ponies with various organizations are also expensive, if you want to do these things.

The important point in all this is to realize that the health and contentment of the pony comes first: it is essential to budget carefully so that we have enough money to call in the vet, or other specialist when he or she is needed and not to hold off and wait because we dread the bill coming in! We must be able to pay feed and bedding bills, to get out of bed early in the morning and perhaps go to bed late at night to check on and care for a pony, or be prepared to pay someone else to do so for us, such as when the pony is boarded out or kept at livery.

Ponies are not toys or bikes. They cannot be pushed into a cupboard and ignored until we feel like playing with them or have time to muck them out, groom them, spend time with them as friends and exercise them properly. The pony must not always come second to school work for both are equally important: if your pony is ill, someone may have to take time off work or school to look after him, like any other member of the family. He is a living, breathing creature who needs as much care and status as any human member of the family even though he does not live in the house with us.

Proper care of a pony is an education itself in responsibility, commitment and sensitivity towards others. He should not be regarded as 'tying', a nuisance or an unwelcome expense, but as a friend and teacher who will repay a thousand times all the care you give him in ways you may never have imagined. Often, you will not appreciate how valuable your pony has been to you until you look back years later and realize what an honour it is to have a pony.

pony types and breeds

All domesticated horses and ponies belong to the species *Equus caballus*. But you'll find, once you get to know your pony, that ponies can be quite different from horses. Ponies are generally quicker-witted, more determined (which can be a good or a bad thing!) and crafty and street-wise, and although they can be mischievous, this does not mean that they are necessarily naughty. Ponies come in all shapes and sizes, and for their size are generally stronger than horses, so the medium to larger ponies can be ridden by lightweight adults who are not too tall. Even ponies which are now too small for you can take up something new, like driving, and so learn a new job which is great fun for everyone.

When does a pony stop being a pony?

There is something in the horse world called 'pony character' which is impossible to describe! It is something you just pick up on being around ponies; they have a certain look about the face and a particular type of personality which makes everyone well aware of the difference between horses and ponies.

As far as height is concerned, technically, a pony is 14.2 hands high or under (which is about 1.47m – see page 11) but, again, the animal must have 'pony character' to be regarded as a pony. Some horses, although smaller than 14.2hh, are *always* described as horses, such as the Arab; despite sometimes being small, the Arab is all horse. The Caspian, which stands no higher than 12hh, is also a horse; but some ponies which should be no taller than 14.2hh (according to their breed society rules) are sometimes taller than that yet are obviously of strong pony character.

TIP: *The most important factor for judging whether or not an equine (a term which also covers zebras and donkeys) is a pony or a horse is character.*

What is a cob?

Another type of animal which is very popular is the cob. Again hard to define, cobs are a distinctive type, not a breed (but see Welsh Cob and Welsh Pony of Cob Type, see page 20), and have a very special personality. Unlike horses and ponies, it is impossible to plan to breed a cob – they just seem to appear now and then! They are very strong, stocky and muscular, heavy-boned but not clumsy and dull, and usually make up to 15.3hh. They make ideal rides for fairly heavy riders. Normally of good temperament, a good cob will look after a rider, whether elderly, novice or nervous. Not being terribly tall, yet stronger than a pony, their height is not off-putting, as a horse's might be, yet they are big and steady enough to give confidence.

poll

hindquarters croup withers muzzle

hock

sheath flank

cannon

knee

fetlock coronet

pastern

How tall is your pony?

Horses, cobs and ponies are all measured in units called 'hands' although metric equivalents are now being more widely used to describe height.

The term 'hand' came about hundreds of years ago when precise height was not regarded as important, as it so often is today, at least in showing and some competitions. A hand is 4in (10cm), the approximate width of a man's hand, so if you want to get a reasonable measurement of your pony use the width of a man's hands to measure him in a vertical line from the highest point of the withers down to the ground - or use a tape measure!

Hands are split into inches, so an animal could be 12 hands 1in, written as 12.1 hands high or 12.1hh. Note that the full stop here is not a decimal point. Another animal might be 14.2hh or 13.3hh or even 13.3 ½hh, meaning 13.3hh plus ½in. The measurement of, say, 11.4hh is never seen because, as there are 4in (10cm) in a hand, this pony would be 12hh. You would say that the above ponies were 'fourteen two' (the words 'hands high' usually being omitted), 'thirteen three' and 'thirteen three and a half', not 'fourteen point two', and so on. If a pony is an exact height, though, say 14hh, you would say 'fourteen hands' or maybe 'fourteen hands high'.

If you want to know the metric measurement, you simply convert the hands measurement into inches, add on any extra inches (up to three) and convert the inches to centimetres (2.5cm to the inch). The answer is usually expressed as 1m and however many centimetres, or occasionally entirely in centimetres.

Above: *A smaller, dappled grey show pony of riding type, beautifully turned out.*

Above right: *This larger type of pony is suitable for the older child.*

Pony types

Most ponies, like dogs, are 'mongrels' although that is not a word used in the horse world. This vast pool of 'ordinary' ponies is where you will most likely find your first and often ideal pony. This type of pony can be intelligent, healthy if reasonably well cared for, hardy and kind-natured. They can do very well in competitions and showing classes where actual breeding is of no importance and, most importantly, this will be the sort of pony with which you will be able to have a great deal of fun.

There are also, at all levels of competition and showing, many ponies which are of no special breed, often of mixed blood, but, unlike those described in the previous paragraph, of clearly defined type usually intended for specific showing classes.

The Show Pony or Riding Pony ponies in this category are often very refined animals, rather like small Thoroughbreds and often have temperaments to match. You have to be very competent to ride this type. However, many have steadier, kinder temperaments than a few years ago. They are full of 'quality' but must not be weedy with spindly legs: the most important thing is that they need to be suitable for a good child rider.

They need a showy appearance and great presence, meaning that you really want to look at them, for success in the show ring where they are shown in classes divided by height. The exact divisions vary

between countries so contact the organization under whose rules you wish to compete for details.

The riding/show pony must have the conformation and action of the near-perfect riding animal with definite pony character and a sensible outlook.

Pony of Hunter Type a more robust type of pony than the show pony, ponies of hunter type must be strong, have a good, flowing, hunting action (although they do not have to jump in the ring) and be workmanlike or handsome rather than pretty or beautiful and elegant. They need excellent manners, to be willing to pull up readily from a fast canter or gallop, a free, well-balanced action and a co-operative nature.

Working Hunter Pony this pony does jump in the ring and must do so in a flowing, unhesitating but sensible style, showing that it can look after a young rider during a day with hounds. Again, a workmanlike appearance is preferred, substantial conformation with quality and a free, well-balanced action. Its manners should be, like the other type categories, impeccable and it must give its rider confidence and a feeling of safety both on the ground and over jumps.

Ponies of all types, but especially the last two categories, often compete in other types of class, too, such as equitation, cross-country, show-jumping and Pony Club and junior Riding Club events.

Above: *Working hunter ponies need to jump in a flowing hunting style.*

Above left: *A small roan show pony going very kindly for his young rider.*

Above, 1: *A grey Welsh Mountain Pony Section A.*

Above right, 2: *An American Pinto Miniature Horse. In the UK and Ireland, this colouring is called piebald.*

Above right, 3: *A chestnut New Forest Pony.*

Above right, 4: *A skewbald pony.*

Above right, 5: *This Welsh Cob Section D is black with white socks.*

Right, 6: *A Welsh Pony of Cob Type Section C. It is bay with white long socks.*

Your pony's colour and markings

Ponies come in all imaginable horsey colours. Anything goes, except in some breed societies which decree that certain colours or markings are not allowed.

The photographs in this book illustrate the great range of colours and markings you will come across. Basically, the darkest colour is black and the palest, snow white.

Ponies are never described as white, always grey unless the pony is an albino pony with no colouring matter in its skin called melanin, which creates the colour. Albinos will have pink skin and white hair and pink or blue eyes.

Black can be sooty or blue-black. Brown coats can be very dark indeed, sometimes to the extent that the pony appears black. In such cases, look at the muzzle area around the mouth: in a brown pony this will be a lighter, beigey colour.

Brown ponies always have dark bodies, sometimes with a slightly lighter belly area, and dark brown manes and tails.

Bay ones have lighter brown bodies with black manes and tails.

Chestnut ponies can range from dark chocolate colour (called liver chestnut) through red chestnut to reddish gold. The mane and tail can match the coat or be darker or lighter. If the mane and tail are very pale, they are called flaxen.

Palomino ponies are a type of very pale chestnut; their bodies should be the colour of a newly-minted gold coin and their manes and tails silver or blonde.

Greys are often born black and lighten gradually to white, or nearly so, in old age. Grey coats are a mixture of white or black and can have different patterns such as mottles called dapples or flecks which designate the pony as a 'flea-bitten' grey. Don't make the mistake of calling it 'moth-eaten'! Grey horses, particularly Arabs, with chestnut hairs are often called rose greys.

Duns have a mixture of coloured hairs with white ones, sometimes giving an almost brindle-like appearance. Duns look yellowish or beige and have usually black manes and tails. If they also have black legs (as with any pony) they are described as having black points. Duns also have a dark stripe running all the way from the poll, down the back to the tail, called an eel stripe or list.

Roans have a mixture of white hairs with black (called blue roans as they look slightly navy-bluish) or with chestnut (when they are called strawberry or rose roans because they look pinkish).

Cream ponies are cream all over, including the mane and tail which match the coat, and they often have blue eyes whereas the normal colour for a pony's eyes is dark brown. If a pony has one blue eye and one brown, the blue one is called a 'wall' eye. This does not affect his eyesight.

Ponies which have large, irregular patches of white plus black are called piebald (black and white – remember magpies and pied wagtails) or skewbalds (any other colour or colours and white). A special breed which has mottles, patches and splashes on its coat is the American breed, the Appaloosa (mainly horses), and there are spotted ponies (white with black, brown or chestnut spots all over).

It is not true that colour influences temperament, or that skewbalds are 'common'. There are special societies for owners of these types, which are called 'coloured' ponies (as if they weren't all coloured!) and many top-class competition ponies have been coloured.

'white bits'

There are several variations of markings, but these are the main ones:

White face A big white patch over almost all the face.

Blaze A slightly narrower patch running down the face.

Snip A white area on the nose.

Stripe A thin patch running down the face.

Star A small white patch on the forehead, which many ponies have.

Sock The white area on the pastern, fetlock and a little way up the leg.

Stocking A white area that reaches higher than a sock – up to, or nearly up to, the knee or hock.

Ermine marks Coloured spots on a white area around the coronet.

Right: *A dappled grey Highland Pony.*

Top: *A chestnut Shetland Pony.*

Middle: *A black Fell Pony.*

Bottom: *A black Dales Pony.*

British and Irish native ponies and cobs

No book about ponies would be complete without a look at these. The British Isles are unique in the world in having many indigenous, or native, pony breeds. 'Native' means the kinds of pony which were living in Britain and Ireland at the time they were cut off from the European land-mass at the end of the last Ice Age, roughly ten to twelve thousand years ago.

Over those thousands of years, though, the native ponies have been mixed with other breeds (often Arab and Thoroughbred horses but sometimes heavy horses, too) which means that they are not 'pure' breeds, and have been exported all over the world. The breeds are as follows.

Shetland Pony a small pony from the very northernmost islands of Scotland, the Shetland is usually measured in inches, not hands, and stands up to 40in (106cm), and is amazingly strong for its height. One pony is said to have carried a man of 12 stones or 168lb (76kg) 40 miles (64km) in one day, but what state it was in at the end of the trip is not known!

The Shetland islands are bleak and bitter and the Shetland Pony grows the thickest coat of all the native breeds, almost like fur and very water resistant. These ponies have strong personalities and, being small and easy and cheap to keep, are sometimes used as companions to excitable competition and racehorses; they find no difficulty in keeping their much bigger charges under strict control.

They are used as first ponies for small children but are actually rather too wide in the back for very small children, having very stocky bodies. They are excellent harness ponies and family pets.

Eriskay Pony this is a very rare pony now, and one of the purest breeds, although thanks to a few enthusiastic breeders it is on the increase again. Science has shown that it is of different ancestry from other natives and further work in this direction will be most interesting. It is very unlikely that you will find an Eriskay Pony on the general market to buy at present.

Highland Pony another Scottish native, the Highland Pony is variable in type because there used to be light and heavier sorts. Nowadays, they are all classed as one breed. Their traditional jobs have been as general farm and estate ponies, used in light haulage, transport and as stalking ponies and, in the past, as mounts and transport ponies for Highland clans and regiments.

Most Highlands are grey and dun with variations of these two colours known as yellow, gold, mouse, fox and cream. 'Ordinary' grey, black, chestnut, bay and brown colours are also found. They come in all sizes up to 14.2hh although the very small, Shetland-size, ones are now uncommon.

They are very kind and co-operative and make ideal family ride-and-drive ponies. They are used extensively for trekking in the Scottish tourist industry.

Dales Pony the Dales Pony comes from the Yorkshire hills and dales on the east of the Pennine Hills which run down the northern half of England. They are strong and energetic, usually black with very little white on the feet and face, and up to 14.2hh. A heavy-ish type of pony, they are excellent for teenagers and small to medium size adults and were in the past used as pack ponies and racing trotters. Today, they make excellent ride-and-drive ponies (ponies which can be both ridden and driven). They come in all colours.

Fell Pony the Fell Pony is an ancestor of the Dales Pony but is smaller and does not exceed 14hh. It comes from the western side of the Pennine Hills where many still run free.

Black is the most common and favourite colour for Fells, but brown, bay and grey occur. White markings are frowned upon although a small star on the forehead is allowed. A very little white is permitted on the feet, but greatly disliked by purist enthusiasts of the breed.

Descended from the Dutch Friesian horse brought to Britannia by the Romans, the Fell has been used in trotting races and for herding sheep and today is used in England's Lake District as a trekking pony for tourists. It is popular as a children's pony and in harness.

New Forest Pony one of the larger British native ponies at up to 14.2hh, New Forest Ponies come from the New Forest in Hampshire, one of England's southernmost counties. The New Forest is now mainly open scrubland and very poor, over-grazed pasture, or boggy moorland, and the ponies living out on it are often in poor condition and are not pure,

Below: *A Pony of The Americas with Appaloosa colouring.*

Pony of the Americas

Like many pony breeds, the Pony of The Americas (the POA) is a composite made up of the blood of the Scottish Shetland Pony, the Appaloosa (based on old Iberian – Spanish/Portuguese – blood), the Quarter Horse (Iberian blood, oriental blood such as Arabian and Barb, Thoroughbred blood and various European types) and direct Arab introductions.

The Shetland and the Appaloosa are very different but the skill of American breeders has produced a lovely, sound, well-balanced pony with a kind temperament suitable for children.

Strict registration and breeding standards are applied to the POA to try to create a miniature horse of Quarter Horse/Arab type.

pedigree New Forest Ponies. Sadly, many are killed each year by tourist drivers who go too fast on the many roads traversing the forest.

The New Forest was created by William the Conqueror in 1072 as a royal hunting reserve although King Canute is said to have ridden local ponies in the area before this. Traditionally, the ponies were used for farming purposes and transport but today the New Forest Pony mainly works as a family riding pony, also going well in harness. It is naturally used for trekking in the forest and is versatile enough to be used as an all-round, talented pony for the whole family.

It can be any colour but 'coloured' (parti-coloured) and blue-eyed cream is also not allowed.

Lundy Pony this pony is descended very largely from the New Forest and has been bred in the Bristol Channel area of southern England, mainly on Lundy Island, for many years more or less as an isolated type. The breed has developed a unique greyish-dun colour. Its characteristics are the same as the New Forest and it is popular as an all-round family pony, although it exists in fairly small numbers.

Exmoor Pony the Exmoor is one of the purest native breeds, having had virtually no outside blood introduced into it. It is very easily recognizable because it is always bay, brown or dun and has a distinctive 'mealy' (oatmeal-coloured) muzzle (the area around the nose and mouth) and the same colour around the eyes, inside the flanks and sometimes under the belly. No white is allowed anywhere and the fore-lock, mane and tail are always black. They stand up to 12.3hh in height.

Exmoors still run free on Exmoor in the south-western 'foot' of Eng-land. The environment and climate are wild and harsh so the ponies, especially those bred on the moor, are hardy, tough, strong and agile.

They are used mainly as children's riding ponies and for trekking. They have great stamina and are used in endurance riding and competi-tive driving trials.

Dartmoor Pony this breed is tough, strong and hardy (able to with-stand bad weather on little food) and has a quiet, sensible and kind nature. It comes from the extreme south west of England, from Dart-moor, which is a bleak, unforgiving landscape with boggy ground, poor keep (grass), and craggy tors (granite outcrops). Some still run wild on Dartmoor.

Oozing pony character, the Dartmoor makes a wonderful child's rid-ing pony or a family driving pony, doing well in competition due to its well-balanced conformation, slender but sturdy legs, natural agility and tough feet. Mainly brown and bay, excessive white markings on the legs and head are discouraged by its breed society. It stands up to 12.2hh.

Connemara Pony this is Ireland's only, and very beautiful, native pony breed, coming from the windswept and romantic west coast of Ire-land. It has a distinctive 'Irish' look about it, as if it has a bit of the leprechaun in it; however, despite being descended from the indigenous Irish type of pony it has a lot of other blood in its veins.

Right: *A Welsh Pony Section C which is brown with white socks.*

Far right: *This light chestnut pony with white socks is a Welsh Cob Section D.*

Left, top: *A Welsh Mountain Pony Section A, which is chestnut with white socks.*

Left, bottom: *This Welsh Pony Section B is dark brown with white socks.*

A well-balanced, level-headed pony, it is known to be a good jumper with excellent conformation, action and stamina. The Connemara makes a good family hunter, being up to 14.2hh. Usually grey, all solid colours (not piebald or skewbald) can be found, including dun with an eel stripe or list down the spine. Traditionally it has been a farm pony used for light work on the land and is used today as an all-round riding and trekking pony, hunter and hack. It is an excellent foundation breed for crossing with the Thoroughbred when producing competition horses.

Welsh Breeds

There are four Welsh breeds: the Welsh Mountain Pony Section A, the Welsh Pony Section B, the Welsh Pony of Cob Type Section C and the Welsh Cob Section D.

The Welsh Mountain Pony the smallest at up to 12hh, and the original Welsh wild pony albeit with other blood in it today. Like all Welsh breeds, it has a spectacular, far-reaching action and an energetic presence which makes it extremely popular in the show ring. Mainly grey, it can be any colour except piebald and skewbald.

Many Welsh Mountain Ponies were used as pit ponies in the past but today they are used almost entirely as children's ponies. Having evolved on the windswept and severe Welsh Hills, they are tough and, like all ponies they are very good doers.

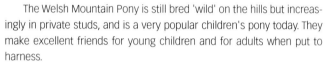

Above: *This pony shows breed colouring typical of all Exmoors.*

Below: *A dun Lundy Pony with dapples and white socks.*

The Welsh Mountain Pony is still bred 'wild' on the hills but increasingly in private studs, and is a very popular children's pony today. They make excellent friends for young children and for adults when put to harness.

The Welsh Pony 'bred up' from the Welsh Mountain Pony and standing up to 13.2hh. Being bigger, it is used more as a children's competition pony but is also very popular in the show ring. Most are bred on studs and, having been formerly used in Welsh slate quarries and as 'surface' (above-ground) ponies in mining, they are now used exclusively as children's ponies and driving ponies. It is a hardy pony, notable for seldom going lame.

The Welsh Pony of Cob Type a small cob up to 13.2hh, only called a pony because of its height. Good ones are 'all cob' in character. It is probably the best ride-and-drive 'pony' there is being smallish yet strong and easily able to pull a vehicle containing parents and two children.

Traditionally, the Welsh Pony of Cob Type worked as a farm and family pony for riding, transport and hunting, herding the sheep and carrying the family to chapel on Sundays. It can easily cope with the rough roads of its native country and is lively, friendly, energetic and easily trained.

Today, it is perfect as a ride-and-drive family pony/cob, an excellent trekking pony and a competent, willing all-rounder.

The Welsh Cob without doubt one of the most impressive members of the equine species, the Welsh Cob's trot, in particular, is stunning. These cobs exude strength, fire, power and pride without arrogance and are a sight once seen never forgotten.

Historically, the Welsh Section D has been used for light farm work, transport, herding under saddle and pulling a cart laden with produce to market: its traditional homeland in recent centuries has been Cardiganshire (Dyfed) and its breeders are known as Cardi Men.

Today, the Welsh Cob is making a name for itself in competition driving trials, as a cross with the Thoroughbred to make a teenager's competition horse and is, as always, an excellent all-round family animal, sure-footed, athletic and easy to keep. Again all colours except piebald and skewbald are permitted and there is no upper height limit although many of the best breeders feel that the Section D loses its true type if it reaches over 15hh.

Through some quirk of fate, no other country in the world has so many indigenous, native breeds as have Great Britain and Ireland. Some are detailed elsewhere but readers may wonder why they are mentioned so often. The reasons are that not only are there so many different breeds coming from such a tiny part of the world but also that they are very varied and superb in type, physique and temperament.

They have been exported to every continent of the world either to breed on as pure-breds or to found national breeds for other countries. In early times when equines were essential for earning a living and running countries (as they still are in some places), small but strong and fast animals were much in demand and Britain and Ireland supplied the world market. Their descendants have thrived, changed somewhat sometimes and now fill a new need as mainly children's ponies or adults' driving ponies all over the world.

Above left: *A brown Dartmoor Pony.*

Below: *A dun Connemara Pony.*

which pony for you?

The most important consideration when buying a pony is always to get one on which you feel safe and which can be relied on to look after you. Although every experienced horse person will agree that there is no such thing as a 'perfect pony', for a first pony you do want one which is nearly so.

What is the perfect pony?

Everyone's idea of the perfect pony differs: very experienced young riders won't mind a few problems so long as the pony will do the job they want – maybe jump athletically round a course of show jumps, or gallop fearlessly around a cross-country course – but if you are a more novice or beginner rider you will certainly be better off with an extremely well-mannered pony, often called a 'patent safety' or 'schoolmaster' pony who knows his or her job thoroughly, will teach you how to go on and generally look after you.

Another term heard is 'bombproof'. This means that the pony will not be startled and unseat you, and will not shy, spook, run away or react badly to such things as sudden loud noises, traffic, aircraft, umbrellas, roadworks, other animals, exciting situations like showgrounds, brass bands, trains and so on. Such ponies do exist and are priceless – even though they are not, of course, 'bombproof'! No horse or pony is.

Above right: *A child's first pony after the leading rein stage should have impeccable manners and be totally trustworthy.*

Left: *Leading rein ponies must be very quiet and well behaved for safety reasons and to encourage young riders.*

Far right: *Having gained confidence on steady ponies, children can progress to more demanding disciplines.*

If you are a young rider you will still be growing, so don't pick a pony who is too small because he will soon seem even smaller as you continue to get taller. When riding a pony, the soles of your boots should not really come below his belly and should be higher than that, with a normal, comfortable stirrup length, if you want to be riding him for a few years.

The second most important point to consider is whether or not you actually like the pony and feel you could be good friends. However tempting, do not go for a glamorous pony which is not kind-natured or which actually bites, kicks or has other nasty tricks just because he looks good. Choose a well-behaved pony with a good temperament who is interested in you, pleasant and easy to deal with and, of course, can do the type of work you want.

How good a rider are you?

If you are already going to a riding school, the instructors there will give you an idea of how good you are and what sort of pony you could cope with. If you do not go to a riding school, it is a good idea to book an assessment lesson at one and tell the staff that you want an idea of how good – or bad! – you are because you are thinking of buying your own pony and want to know what level of ability you should be looking for in the pony.

Always choose a riding stable which is approved by the relevant national or state organization (The Association of British Riding Schools (ABRS) or The British Horse Society (BHS) in the UK). Schools which have been approved will usually display a plaque to indicate this.

Above: *Older, more competent children are ready, with good teaching, to handle more difficult ponies, although this one looks very co-operative.*

How are you going to keep your pony?

There are various ways of keeping ponies ranging from keeping them stabled all the time (a very poor and even cruel system) to their living out 'at grass' (in a field) all the time (which can also be cruel if the pony is not well cared for and given good shelter). As in everything, there is a happy medium.

Stabled

If you are a competent rider and wish to buy an accomplished competition pony, probably with a good deal of Arab or Thoroughbred blood in it, the pony will almost certainly need to be stabled at least at night in winter and during the day in a hot, fly-ridden summer. Arabs and Thoroughbreds are classed as 'hot blooded' horses often used in breeding quality, athletic ponies able to win in the show ring, jump 'serious' courses or compete in dressage, and they cannot withstand being out all the time in extreme weather conditions – either wind, rain and snow or under blazing sun with lots of flies.

At grass

Ponies and cobs which are all native in their breeding, or very nearly so, can usually live out very healthily, and much more happily, all year round provided they have good shelter. Even tough natives don't like too much hot sun, flies or driving wind and steady rain.

They are best kept on poorish grazing, the sort used for sheep or non-milking cattle, and even then may need to have their grazing restricted to a very few hours a day to avoid health problems. Such ponies will need other accommodation such as stabling, yarding or a non-grass turnout area.

Combined system

This is the best way to keep your pony because it is very flexible and adaptable to your changing yearly routine – your pony is stabled for some of the time, and out at grass for some of the time.

Again, depending on the type and/or breed of pony you get, it is normally a good plan to stable ponies at night in the winter and during the day in summer. This keeps them out of the worst weather and in the best living conditions at both times of the year. In winter they can come in to a clean, deep bed with plenty of hay and water and possibly a feed, and in summer they can rest indoors away from sun and flies, but their stables *must* be well ventilated and made of materials which do not cause them to become stiflingly hot and stuffy in hot weather. (See page 39.)

take care – don't overfeed

Most ponies and cobs cannot take rich grazing. This sort of lush grass can make them dangerously fat or actually ill, usually with a potentially fatal disease called laminitis, the old name for which was fever in the feet (see page 156). One cause of this is too much food and it is particularly common in ponies and cobs who are given too much rich grazing, especially in spring when the grass is high in sugar, but also to a lesser extent in summer and autumn.

Left: *Getting out and about: this palomino pony is looking after its young rider very well and cantering along quietly.*

Yarding

This is another system which is probably better than either stabling or being at grass without shelter. Ponies are kept together in a large, covered building or pen rather than in individual stables or outdoors. Usually the floor is bedded down with straw or shavings, or with a 'riding-type' ground surface such as earth, woodchips or, more rarely, bark or even sand or a synthetic, maybe plastic granule, surface. The building will have a roof over at least part of it, and there may be a surfaced, fenced-in pen in front of it into which the ponies can come and go. Ideally it will open on to a field so that they can be either indoors or outdoors as they wish.

TIP: *Only ponies which are friendly towards each other should be kept in this way so that fights do not break out and ponies become injured. In these circumstances, ponies have company, shelter and freedom and it is an ideal way of housing them*.

Livery

Most people who have ponies do not have their own land and stables; they keep them at what is called 'livery' in yards (the word commonly used for horse premises), either riding schools or pure livery stables.

Usually, keeping a pony at livery involves renting a stable and grazing and maybe also paying the staff to do

◆ all the work (full livery);
◆ some of the work with you doing the rest (part livery); or
◆ with you doing all the work (Do-It-Yourself livery).

Some arrangements include all the pony's feed and bedding; with others you buy it separately.
There is also an option in some riding schools called working livery, when the pony is allowed to be used in riding school lessons for clients and so the livery fee is lowered. This is not a brilliant plan because the riding school normally wants the pony at the same times as you (weekends and evenings) and the pony can be spoiled by having lots of riders; everyone rides in a slightly different way. If only competent riders and/or staff ride him this may work if you can both agree on scheduling his working times. No matter how cheap the livery, it is no good if the pony is overworked or never available when you want him.

Keeping a pony at home

For this, you need grazing and some kind of shelter – either a stable, preferably arranged so that the pony can come in and out as necessary, or a shed where he can stand away from weather and flies – a water source, somewhere to keep your tack and feed and another horse or pony for company. Ponies are herd animals and most of them are miser-

Below: *This skewbald/coloured pony is a larger, more substantial type, which is ideal for older children and teenagers.*

able on their own, and can develop problems such as trying to escape, bad behaviour, wrecking the stable or just being so unhappy that they are never really healthy.

You also need to be sure that there are no planning restrictions preventing you from keeping the pony at home, or from building new stables and 'ancillary buildings' such as tack and feed stores, or converting existing buildings into stables. Sometimes you may not even graze a pony on a paddock which has formerly been used for, say, agricultural animals; this would involve a change of use because ponies are not classed as agricultural animals. You will have to check everything very carefully with your local authority.

What you can do with your pony

There are lots of activities in which you and your pony can take part. The best reason for buying a pony is simply because you love ponies and want a friend to look after, ride and have fun with.

Taking part in competition is all well and good and can be great fun provided you keep winning in perspective, but it is not the main reason for buying a pony. Ponies are flesh and blood and their welfare is always of far more importance than winning prizes; you can easily have fun competing and also have a healthy, happy pony who is well cared for and loved.

Show-jumping

For show-jumping you need a controllable, athletic pony who doesn't 'hot up' (become excited) during his round. He must increase and decrease speed when asked, turn nimbly and, at least for the higher levels, needs a natural jumping ability.

There are all sorts of show-jumping events, ranging from those affiliated to a show-jumping society such as the British Show Jumping Association in the UK to informal competitions which you can enter for fun and practice and maybe win a rosette, a trophy or a small amount of prize money. The Pony Club in the UK (or the 4H Club in the United States) and local riding clubs also organize show-jumping competitions, as do horse shows of all levels and types.

The fences are coloured, and the courses carefully designed and built with both safety and the level of ability of pony and rider in mind. Sometimes you compete against the clock in a jump-off to decide the winner and sometimes the height of the fence is the decider. Ponies do need to be reasonably fit for show-jumping, but even fitter for cross-country.

Cross-country

Cross-country competitions may be 'stand-alone' ones such as hunter trials or practice courses, or they may be part of eventing (involving dressage, show-jumping and cross-country) or combined training (involving dressage and show-jumping only).

Ponies need to be quite fit to gallop across country and jump 'rustic' (non-painted, natural-looking) fences and the sport is very exhilarating. To be successful, a pony needs a natural turn of speed and good jumping ability – and the rider needs to be pretty brave with a good deal of 'stickability' because some of the fences involve drops, water, ditches and combined hazards such as roads and streams, and there may be banks and other obstacles.

The British Horse Trials Association organizes eventing (horse trials) in the UK, and cross-country competitions of various sorts are also organized by the Pony Club (4H Club) and riding clubs, or the bigger riding centres.

Above: *Show/stadium jumping is a very precise sport needing good training and calm competition temperament in both pony and rider.*

Left: *A willing, well-trained pony is just what you need for developing confidence and jumping skills.*

Hunting

This is not a competitive sport, but you need a fit pony nevertheless. You can hunt 'proper' when the hounds will pursue a live animal (for example, a fox or hare) or you can drag-hunt in which hounds follow a specially man-laid scent and no live animal is chased or killed.

It is quite possible to go out hunting and not jump a single fence. There are plenty of gates and lots of people do not jump so it is entirely up to you.

If there is a local hunt you will surely know about it. Following a hunt involves a strict code of conduct known as 'hunting etiquette' which must be followed if you do not want to risk a public telling off by a hunt official, usually the Field Master (who controls the followers – known as the field) or even the Master himself. This is always a disgrace! Your pony *must* be good with hounds and dogs as it is a heinous crime for a horse or pony to kick or trample a hound.

It has to be said that some pretty awful riders go out hunting, so you don't need to worry that you are not good enough! Your pony, however, does need to be at least moderately fit as you are often mounted for several hours which is wearying to the pony and hard on his back, and he may spend a lot of time galloping and jumping.

Dressage

Dressage is a French word meaning simply 'training'. Unfortunately, it has come to be seen as a competitive activity in its own right which has lost its original meaning. Dressage tests started simply as a test of the standard of training of a horse and rider but are now seen as competitive first and educational second.

Dressage ponies today need a straight, extravagant action at the higher levels to impress the judges. At lower levels, accuracy and a correct way of going get good marks but sadly many judges do not make allowances for a pony's natural action according to his type and breed. No Exmoor Pony, for example, can possibly go as extravagantly as a Thoroughbred-cross pony with more scope, and should be marked for going as well and accurately as he can, but this is usually not the case. So for dressage at higher levels you usually need a pony with some Thoroughbred or warmblood in him and, for children's ponies, a dash of Arab blood adds style and elegance.

Competitions are run by local dressage groups, the Pony Club (4H Club), riding clubs and other organizers such as riding centres.

Showing

This must be one of the most popular equestrian activities ever! Shows run from early spring (often indoors) to late autumn and every weekend is crammed with fixtures advertised in horse magazines.

There are classes such as those for ponies of a specific breed (full and part bred, in-hand/at halter or ridden), types (see pages 12–13) such

Above: This palomino pony and rider are working in at a show. Showing is one of the most popular equestrian sports.

as Riding/Show Pony, Hunter Type, Working Hunter, and the ever-popular Equitation classes in which the rider, not the pony, is judged. There are Competition Pony classes, Family Pony classes, Handy Pony classes, Veteran classes usually for ponies over 15 years of age, Best Turned Out classes in which the clothing and tack are judged along with the neatness of plaiting, trimming and so on, side-saddle classes and all sorts of novelty classes such as fancy dress.

You can show in 'unaffiliated' shows and classes which are not under the control of any particular organization, or can gain points towards a regional or national championship by showing in classes affiliated to breed societies or major organizations (such as the British Show Pony Society in the UK).

In showing, there is truly something for everyone. Adults come into their own in showing even small ponies because almost any pony can be shown in-hand (at halter) in the right class and small adults can enter any pony class with no age restrictions.

Driving

This is another activity in which both children and adults can compete on equal terms because ponies can pull any suitable vehicle no matter who is in it. There are, of course, junior and adult classes and you can drive at shows in breed classes or the very elegant Private Driving Classes and *Concours d'Elégance* classes in which turnout is crucial. Hackney Ponies, a very specialized field, were once crowd-puller classes but are now rarer but equally suitable for children or adults.

In competitive driving trials, the ponies are very efficient and they obviously enjoy the various tasks and atmosphere of the different phases of the competition, such as the cross-country and the dressage/obstacle phase.

Scurry driving against the clock is also very popular and a regular crowd-pleaser at the major indoor winter shows.

If you do not wish to compete in driving, many driving clubs hold regular non-competitive rallies and drives around the countryside, so there is something for everyone. Of course, there is also the driving equivalent of hacking – just getting together with family, friends, or just you and your dog and going out for a drive with your pony and trap for fun and relaxation.

Hacking

Thousands of pony owners just own a pony to love him and look after him and only want to be 'Happy Hackers', simply riding around the lanes and riding tracks for the pleasure of it. This activity teaches you about the countryside, makes it essential that you train your pony properly so that he is safe on public highways and byways in traffic and with farm machinery, and is interesting and stimulating for both you and your pony.

mounted games

Mounted games and gymkhanas are popular events and equestrian organizations put them on. The individual and team competitions are intended as tests of speed and skill and involve such games as getting the most potatoes in a bucket, picking up 'wounded soldiers' and bringing them back to base, obstacle courses and sack races leading one's pony. The word gymkhana comes from a combination of the word gymnastics and the Hindustani gend-Khana which means sports ground.

your pony's home

It is not always easy to find good enough accommodation in which to keep a pony. Just any old field, any old shed or any old yard will not do if you have his welfare and safety at heart. Let's look at fields first because most ponies are healthier and better behaved if they live out most or even all of the time.

field checklist

Avoid a field with puddles or lakes of water on it, or one where the earth is cracked in dry weather.

Look out for clumps of rounded, spiky marsh grasses, or lots of weeds which ponies won't eat such as docks or thistles.

Beware poisonous plants such as ragwort which has clumps of large, yellow, daisy-like flowers which can kill your pony.

Grass for ponies should not be the very rich sort of the kind that dairy cattle need.

Ponies do best on the sort of grassland kept for sheep, dry cows or young cattle.

Remember that you may have to restrict your pony's grazing if you are to avoid laminitis and stop him getting overweight.

Fields

If you want grass to form the main part of your pony's diet – and it is natural to him, after all – you will need a field of roughly 1 hectare or 2 acres for one pony with half that much again for each additional pony, remembering that ponies need company. You can divide up the land into two or three paddocks if it is not split already and rest it on a rota basis, using each paddock in turn during the grazing season for a few weeks, then moving the ponies on to a fresh one whilst the first receives maintenance treatment (see page 70).

The field must be well drained. If it is too wet, it will be waterlogged or desperately muddy in wet weather and so probably out of use, and if it is a clay soil (very fine particles of soil, sticky and thick) it will also bake hard and crack in summer and produce very little grass, all of which are bad for ponies. Sandy soils (large particles, gritty and easily broken up) drain very well in winter but become too dry for grass to grow in summer. Most soils are in between these extremes.

Shelter

This is very important and often overlooked. In summer, ponies become very distressed by flies which never leave them alone, crawling on all their sensitive parts, constantly buzzing and sometimes biting, which can cause skin problems. Some natural shelter such as clumps of trees, shrubbery and thick, high hedges on the windward side of the field (the side from which the wind usually blows) are a big help but the ideal is either a proper field shelter, access into and out of their stables or into an open barn or other covered area out of the hot sun and away from flies in summer and away from wind and continuous rain in winter.

Left: *It is vital not to stable ponies for too long. Most do better if given several hours a day out, with company, on poor grazing.*

natural water supplies

If there are ponds or streams in the field, make sure that they have safe, gently sloping approaches and have the water checked regularly for purity as pollutants can make your pony seriously ill. It is best not to rely on natural supplies as a water source: in winter, ponds, dykes and even streams can freeze over and then the ice can collapse when ponies try to walk on it – many ponies have been injured or drowned this way.

Water

This is essential for all living things and ideally water will be piped to your pony's field into a self-filling trough which automatically fills as the ponies empty it. You can also have large, synthetic containers or simply plastic dustbins filled by hosepipe and tied to the fence, if necessary. Whatever you use must be kept full and clean and have no sharp edges on which the ponies could injure themselves. The containers must also be low enough for ponies to drink from comfortably otherwise they may go short of water.

The land around water sources often becomes very muddy so you can avoid this by laying down sand, shavings, woodchips, straw or something similar. Never use bricks or rubble which can cut ponies' feet.

Company

Very few ponies are happy living alone, and the best company is another, friendly pony (or several) although some graze alongside with donkeys, goats, sheep or cattle. Ponies kept alone are often miserable; they may injure themselves trying to jump out of their fields and can become difficult to handle in the presence of other ponies.

Ponies often play about and can be quite rough with each other but provided there is no actual bullying or serious biting and kicking, ponies are better off in a herd. Definite bullies, though, should be removed from the field for safety.

Security

Anyone who loves their pony must think hard about this. You could ask your local police crime prevention officer to come and look at your premises (if they are your own) and advise on ways to put off thieves and vandals. When looking for livery premises, ask them what security precautions they take.

TIP: *It is strongly advised that your pony be freeze-marked and/or microchipped in his neck so that he can be traced should he escape or be stolen*.

Right: Contrary to popular opinion, ponies are happier if they can see and touch their friends next door – provided they are friends, of course.

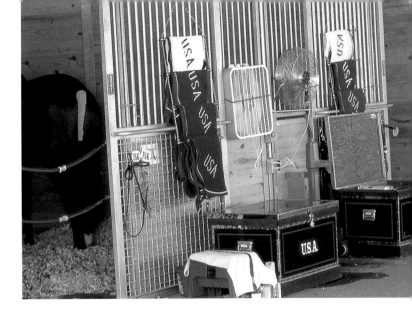

Tack rooms in particular must be securely lockable because tack is valuable and often stolen. All gates to the premises should be locked when not in use and no more gates than necessary should open on to public roads.

A pony's legal owner is responsible for any damage he may do should he get loose, therefore it is vital that the field's fencing and hedges are strong and high enough to prevent his escape. They should be at least the height of the pony's back and preferably higher, and be free of sharp edges, nails, screws, sharp bolts and barbed wire which can seriously injure horses.

Thick, high, prickly hedges are ideal, as are wooden posts and rails which are traditionally used for horses and ponies. Posts with very taut, strained, plain wire can be good. Never use barbed wire. Sheep fencing, too, is dangerous because ponies always seem to get their hooves through it and can either panic and pull the whole thing down, rip their shoes off (so damaging their hooves) or otherwise injure themselves trying to get free. Alternatively, they may give up and stand trapped in the fence, unable to eat, drink or shelter and also be at the mercy of bullies and vandals until someone arrives to check on them.

Gates should similarly be strong and high and preferably filled in on their bottom halves with strong metal mesh (not weak wire netting) to prevent ponies getting their legs through the bars which may happen if ponies are milling around waiting for someone to visit.

Stables

Stables are often too small and too stuffy. Ponies are active and need to be able to move around, lie down, roll, sleep flat out and get up again in safety. In small stables in particular, ponies may become 'cast' (stuck with their legs folded against the wall, quite unable to get up) and can injure themselves or die from struggling, exhaustion or pneumonia as the lung on the side on which they are lying slowly fills with body fluids.

A reasonable size of stable for a 12.2hh pony is about 2.4m or 8ft square, whereas one of 14.2hh will feel comfortable in one about 3.6m or 12ft square. Ponies do need space above their heads too so, for a 13.2hh pony, aim for a roof or ceiling height of about 2.1m or 7ft.

Ventilation is very important as ponies have sensitive lungs and must have fresh air if they are to remain healthy. A door and window on only one side of the stable is not good enough: there should be air outlets on other walls. Ponies are also happier when they have more than one outlook from their stable.

Most ponies are much happier when they can see and actually touch the pony next door over the interior partition. They are herd animals, after all, so this is understandable. Obviously, only friends should be stabled next to each other whether they can touch or not, otherwise the less dominant pony will always be worried about his aggressive neighbour.

The stable should be light, airy and large enough for your pony, who should at least be able to see and preferably touch his neighbours. Stables for ponies often have the doors too high, forcing them to struggle to look out. This causes pain and strain to the neck and back which can even lead to problems during work. The door should come just above where his neck meets his chest, for comfort. If too low, he may try to jump out.

The floor should be non-slip, the most common material being roughened concrete. Wood is slippery, weak and dangerous, earth can be good if well maintained, and tarmac is occasionally used. Rubber mats are often used these days but are not recommended (see page 89).

Storage

Bedding materials such as baled shavings can often be kept outdoors, saving valuable storage space; if the bags are punctured or torn it does not really matter so long as the material inside can be kept dry and does not go mouldy from damp. Mouldy bedding and feed cause serious lung and digestive diseases in ponies.

Feed room

There must be enough storage space for your pony's feed, hay (and possibly bedding), and this must be dry and kept clean and tidy with spilled food swept up so as not to attract vermin. Make sure that your hay and straw is kept under cover and not exposed to rain which can ruin it.

Keep your pony's feed in galvanized metal bins or strong plastic ones with securely fixed lids, to keep it dry and impossible for loose ponies to get at! Gorging on feed-room supplies has made many a pony seriously ill with colic or laminitis (see page 156). Feeds which come in plastic bales should be opened and fed in accordance with the instructions on the bale. Baled feeds are often double wrapped and can be kept outdoors unless the sacks have ventilation holes which may let in moisture.

covered yards

These are an ideal way of accommodating several friendly ponies, particularly if they have access to an outdoor area or grazing as well. They must be light and airy with no sharp edges or nails on which ponies can hurt themselves.

If the land is exceptionally hard or wet, it may be necessary to provide other turnout facilities and most yards have an outdoor schooling area used for this. Some sort of fenced-off 'play pen', at any rate, must be provided in such circumstances because it is not good to keep ponies permanently stabled, even if they are regularly exercised.

Above: *Housing ponies in a covered barn (called yarding) is ideal as they have more space and close company with other ponies.*

Right: *Feeding is the single most important subject you need to know about when caring for ponies, so learn all you can about it.*

Left: *Tack is valuable so it should be stored and looked after in a dry, warm room.*

Far right, top: *Many people allow rugs to become damp and dirty. Proper rug racks help to keep rugs aired and in good shape.*

Far right, bottom: *Space-saving equipment allows you to keep your gear all together, where you can find it easily, while taking up the minimum amount of valuable space.*

Tack room

This is an important room on any yard because good tack is expensive and must be stored properly. It must be a dry room because damp rots leather and natural fabrics, which must be at about room temperature (roughly 20°C/68°F). The tack room must be well-built with metal bars on the windows and a strong, securely lockable door. If not, it may be safer to take your saddle and bridle home with you after each visit.

Saddles must be stored on proper saddle racks or brackets if they are to keep their shape and bridles must be hung by the headpiece on semi-circular brackets. If they are just hung on narrow pegs or, worse, nails, the headpiece will soon develop a crease or crack.

Rugs and blankets are best kept hung on special rug hangers or brackets so that they can air, and boots and bandages can be stored in drawers, crates or on shelves so long as they are raised off the floor and can be kept clean.

Washing facilities

These are abysmal in most yards! There really should be somewhere for rugs, blankets, numnahs, bandages, boots, gloves and so on to be washed correctly and dried quickly so that:

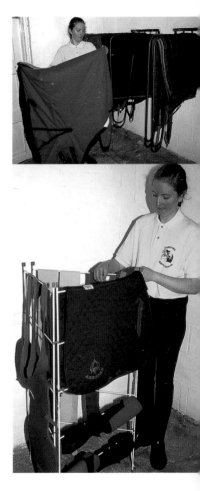

◆ you are not tempted to let your pony stand in filthy clothing all winter because washing it is inconvenient; and

◆ ponies are not forced to wear dirty, damp clothing which is uncomfortable and bad for their health.

Turnout rugs spend most of their time wet and muddy in winter and you really need two per pony so that one can be dried and brushed off each night whilst the second one is in use. You will have to take clothing home and wash it regularly, or perhaps (which is more expensive) have it cleaned often by a horse-clothing laundry.

Riding areas

Unless you only want to hack out, your yard will need some sort of prepared riding area, called a manège if outdoors or an indoor school if in a building. The normal minimum size for a riding area is 40m x 20m (130ft x 60ft). Outdoor areas can be carefully planned and managed turf areas, manèges surfaced with wood chips, synthetic surfaces, rubber, sand or a mixture of these and indoor ones are usually of wood chips and sand mixed, although there are several different surfaces.

The surface must provide cushioning for the ponies' legs (and for when you fall off!), be non-slip and not prone to freezing over, shifting during fast work or jumping or when horses are turned loose on it for exercise, or to becoming waterlogged in wet weather. Creating a really good outdoor riding surface can be very expensive and some yards even restrict clients' use of them to delay replacement costs.

Indoor schools can get really dusty and usually need regular watering either by sprinkler system or hosepipe – with a student or volunteer on the other end!

Some establishments have their own land with tracks on which you can ride. If not, and you want to hack out, you will need to be in an area where there are several riding tracks and, because it is almost impossible to reach these without going on roads, you will also need a traffic-proof pony to get you both there and back in one piece. Often, it is impossible to avoid main roads, too, but if you are a novice you should never hack out alone – make sure you go out with a more experienced rider.

Right: *It is important for peace of mind to sign a proper livery/boarding agreement, so that you know exactly where you stand.*

Livery agreements and insurance

Many well-run livery yards do not ask you to sign any kind of written agreement which makes it clear to both yard owner and you what is expected from each, but it is always safer to have such an agreement in case of accidents, damage to or by the pony, loss of equipment, injury and so on.

Insurance

Firstly, the yard owner, you and your pony must all be covered by appropriate insurance. The yard owner should have insurance to cover for any accidents, personal injury or theft that occur on the yard. You should have insurance to cover you against claims by third parties in the event of injury or damage caused by your pony. Personal accident insurance is also advisable, as is cover for veterinary fees in case of expensive disease or injury and some owner's cover for the cost of the pony should he have to be destroyed or for 'loss of use' should he become incapacitated to the extent that he cannot perform the work for which he was purchased.

Livery agreements

The agreement need not be complicated. It should state:
- exactly what services and facilities are to be provided;
- the cost of these services and facilities;
- when bills are to be paid;
- what extras, if any, you will have to pay for separately;
- that the yard owner may call the vet (veterinarian), if necessary, should your pony suddenly become sick or injured and that you will pay the vet's bill.

There are other clauses which may be included: the important point is to be sure you feel that the agreement is fair to both of you. Once it is signed, you have a deal.

You will also need to give the yard owner fullest details of your pony and his needs, likes and dislikes, vaccination dates, worming dates and so on, plus several phone numbers where you and your family can be reached in an emergency.

Some yard owners are unreasonably controlling over their clients who may sign up because they feel they have nowhere else to go. Some make their clients buy all feed and bedding from them even if it does not suit the pony, many deny grass turnout in winter which can be a big problem when you are at school and cannot exercise every day. Some restrict grazing to very limited periods at other times of year, and others insist that you use their vet, farrier and instructor which, again, is most unreasonable. Try to avoid taking your pony to this kind of yard.

Others are much fairer and at larger yards or riding schools which take liveries you may find that you have free use of the indoor school, a lesson a week, use of the jumps and so on. Carefully read any agreement, ask a responsible person to check it for you, and make sure you are happy with it before anyone signs anything.

Finding the right yard

You can find a suitable yard by looking in your local directories or, most often, by asking other pony owners or local instructors. When you have found a few likely candidates, ring to make an appointment to see round the place.

By far the most important thing is that the horses, ponies and other animals look happy, in good condition (neither too fat nor too thin) and interested in visitors (you) not only for what you might have in your pockets – although a healthy horsey interest in food is to be expected!

The place must look and smell reasonably clean but it does not have to be immaculate. A bit of straw here and there or peeling paintwork is unimportant provided the general air is of a well-maintained, cared-for place.

The staff and, ideally, the other clients should be friendly, not superior or arrogant or with a 'couldn't-care-less' attitude towards you. You must feel at ease with them and feel that you could easily go to them with a problem; if you don't, how can you trust them with your precious pony?

Approval schemes

In the UK, the British Horse Society and the Association of British Riding Schools both run approval schemes for riding schools and the BHS has a scheme for livery stables. In other countries, national, state or regional organizations may also run similar schemes. Local libraries and sports councils are a useful source, worldwide, of groups, societies and other organizations which administer different activities and sports and should be able to provide a starting point for getting relevant information.

Looking around a yard

Don't be afraid to ask lots of questions! The yard owner will want to create a good impression but you want to know about any possible faults, and a line has to be drawn somewhere because no yard is perfect.

Below: Keeping the muck heap reasonably tidy is an important chore!

The important points to check are:

◆ whether there are grass turnout facilities all year round except in freak conditions.

◆ what arrangements are made for freedom if the land really is too bad to use. Keeping ponies stabled full-time without even access to a surfaced riding area for exercise is not acceptable.

◆ what the security arrangements are like.

◆ what the riding facilities are both on the yard and in the surrounding district.

◆ which would be your pony's stable and if he does not get on with his neighbours could a change be made.

◆ whether or not there is someone on the premises round the clock, that is, does someone live on the yard or is it deserted at night? Yards without living accommodation for owner or staff are always a bad security risk.

You have to use your instinct as to whether or not you feel, deep inside, that the yard will be right for you. Try not to get carried away by your enthusiasm at becoming a pony owner if it is your first time: choosing the wrong yard can cause you months of heartache before you eventually find somewhere else. If there is anything at all you are unhappy about, ask about it and try to get a satisfactory explanation, then discuss it with your family and experienced friends before making your decision. Just because a yard has a place, it does not mean that you have to take it.

Above: Ponies must be happy if they are to stay well behaved and healthy. These two friends are 'mutual grooming' which bonds friendship between them.

Keeping your pony at home

If this is your first pony, no matter how perfect he is, keeping him at your home could be risky. There is a very great deal involved in looking after a pony, not least in knowing what not to do and in learning to understand when he is not well or plainly unhappy. There will be no one on hand to ask when things go wrong – and if you are a novice owner you may not even realize things *have* gone wrong. In these circumstances, it is certainly best for you to keep the pony for at least a year at a good, professional livery yard or riding school so that you can gain experience of looking after him at all times of year and in varying circumstances. Then, when you are more competent, take him home.

If you are more experienced and you have the right facilities and proper company for the pony, then go ahead. Keeping a pony outside your own back door is far less tying than keeping him on DIY livery on someone else's place. You can arrange your routine to fit in with your other commitments and are not tied to being at the yard, for example, to feed just because someone else has decreed that feeding time is 5pm, or find that you cannot ride in the school/manège because there are half a dozen ponies loose on it.

On the other hand, you need to make proper arrangements with reliable people to have the pony, and his companion, looked after when you are sick or away. On these occasions, many people send their ponies away on temporary livery. You have to think ahead to plan for all these occasions.

Your premises will also need to be approved for access by large vehicles such as fire engines, ambulances or a horsebox or trailer should the pony have an accident or, if the worst comes to the worst, has to be put down at home and his body removed. Not a nice thought, but it has to be considered.

Many people do keep their ponies very satisfactorily at home, and if you can do so you will find that your relationship with your pony becomes close and rewarding.

Below: *This stable door is far too high for its small occupant to look over comfortably. He will have to strain to see over it which is unpleasant for him and may damage his neck and back.*

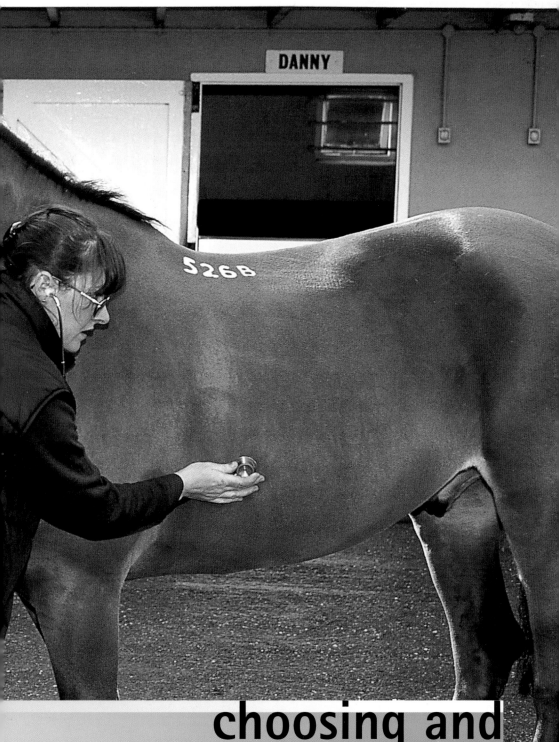

DANNY

526B

choosing and buying your pony

Once you have made the decision to buy a pony and know where you will keep him, there are various ways of finding and buying a pony: you can browse through the advertisements in horsey magazines or contact a dealer with a good reputation. If an opportunity comes up, you could buy a pony you already know, perhaps one belonging to a friend or your riding school. You might perhaps buy one you hear about on the grapevine or which you know about in the district. Another alternative would be to buy a pony at an auction.

Where to look

Each of the ways of finding and buying a horse has its advantages and disadvantages. Below are some suggestions for things to watch out for.

Dealers

Probably the most reliable way of finding a pony suitable for you is to buy one from a good dealer (ask local horse owners). They are usually adept at matching ponies and owners and you should nearly always be able to exchange the pony if things don't work out. However, watch out because the dealer will normally give you less for the pony than you paid, to cover his or her time and trouble plus your having used the pony for a while, so this can prove expensive, especially if a few changes are involved.

Good, professional dealers are covered by insurance and their sales agreements can be quite complicated affairs – whereas others have no agreements at all! Be quite frank with a dealer about:

◆ how the pony will be kept (you don't want a largely Arab or Thoroughbred pony if you can only offer field accommodation);
◆ what you want him for (it's no good complaining that he won't jump if you said you only wanted a dressage pony); and
◆ how good a rider/driver/handler you are (if you are competent you can expect to be regarded as able to handle a more difficult pony, whereas a real novice has to have a virtually 'perfect' pony).

Above right: *Taking an expert advisor with you to examine a prospective pony will put your mind at ease.*

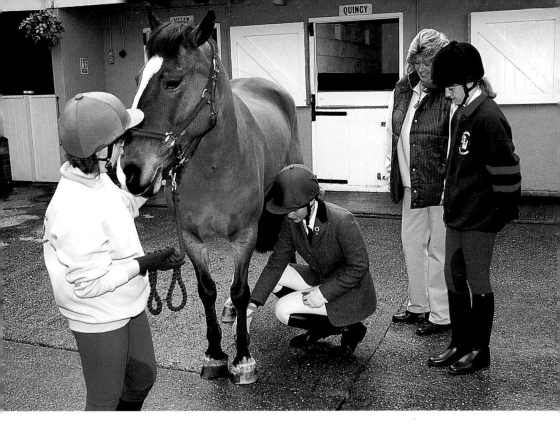

Buying from a friend

Buying a pony you already know, either from a friend, riding school or one you have seen round and about, gives you a head start because you already know quite a bit about him. However, if things go wrong and the pony turns out to be a big disappointment, or you find that he is not quite the animal you were led to believe (not always illegal if it is carefully done!) it can very quickly ruin a beautiful friendship.

TIP: *Get to know as much as possible about such a pony before trying him out and be very sure that he is what you want. Do not let a friend or acquaintance pressurize you into buying a pony you do not really think is for you after all.*

Advertisements

This can be very risky and very disappointing, but you may just come up with an absolute dream. Private sellers sometimes say all sorts of things about their ponies which, when you actually get to their yard to try the pony, are plainly untrue and you have wasted time and money travelling there.

They are also not bound to take back the pony if he turns out to be unsuitable so you must be careful and sure that you have made the right decision. However, if the pony really is good you might lose him if you dither because the seller will not be short of other buyers; but it is more important to take your time and not be panicked into buying too quickly.

help!

Help is what you need when you are buying a pony if you are at all inexperienced. There are professionally qualified people who may be instructors or consultants and who are willing, for a fee, to help you find and choose a suitable pony.

Contact freelance instructors who advertise locally, people involved in the equestrian sport in which you want to take part, riding school owners or staff. Settle on the fee, tell them exactly what you want and be guided by them – remembering that this is to be *your* pony and you must go for the one you feel will be a good friend to you.

Auctions

Most people would tell a novice never to buy a pony at an auction because you have no idea what you are buying. This can be true, but at reputable sales you can inspect and sometimes try ponies first and you have a set time in which to return a pony should he prove to be unsuitable. On the whole, it is far more satisfactory to buy from other sources, even though you may possibly, if you are fortunate, get a nice pony cheaply at an auction.

Making a short list

If you have several ponies to see, make a short list putting the one you like most at the top, and arranging to go and see him or her first. It is usual to be sent a photograph and perhaps also a video tape of the pony. If someone sends you details of a pony you feel is unsuitable, send back any photos or video tapes at once – it is not fair to keep the seller hanging on.

When you and your advisor have decided on a pony or ponies, ring the seller and arrange an appointment – and if you find you cannot keep it ring him or her as soon as possible to rearrange another time.

TIP: *Whenever you go to see a pony with a view to buying him, always take an experienced person with you. Two heads are better than one, and it is essential not to 'fall in love at first sight' with the first pony you see, who may in fact be unsuitable for you. Your advisor will help you to keep your feet on the ground and not rush into anything.*

Trying him out

You and your advisor will probably want to see the pony loose in the field first, to see how he goes naturally and to check whether or not he is easy to catch, and a reasonable seller will understand this. Often the pony will already be up and stabled, cleaned up and looking his best to impress you.

You want a pony who looks interested to see you and is pleased to meet you and looks like good company. If this is your first pony or you are a novice, you do not want one with temperament problems such as biting, threatening behaviour, turning his tail to you when you go into the box and/or threatening to kick, and so on. This is not 'perfect pony' behaviour.

You should see the pony ridden by his normal rider first before you try him yourself to check his usual behaviour. Also ask to see him ridden out on the road, alone and in company if possible (there is nothing worse than a pony who won't do anything without another pony by his side!), and check how he behaves in traffic, how willing he is to leave home and whether or not he charges back too fast.

Note how co-operative he is over being handled, tacked up, untacked, rugged up if appropriate, turned out and perhaps caught again. Remember, though, that many ponies do not want to come in again very soon after they have been turned out – but the perfect pony will not object!

Above left: *Watch the pony's usual rider ride him, so that you can tell how the pony normally goes and behaves.*

Top and above: *Ask to handle, and perhaps tack up, the pony yourself to see if he is kind towards strangers and good to handle.*

Right: *Observe the pony ridden alone and in traffic. It is essential that he goes willingly without other ponies, and does not play up in traffic.*

Bill of Sale

This document, which should be perused by a solicitor to check for accuracy of wording and so on, states that you have paid so much for this particular pony which makes him your legal pony with effect from the date of signature.

  You also need his pedigree, registration and identification papers if he is of a particular breed or registered with any equestrian organization, his freeze-mark papers (the company must be notified of change of ownership), his microchip documents for the same purpose if he is 'chipped' and anything else which goes with him such as vaccination certificates.

When it is your turn to ride, drive or handle the pony, be confident, fair, relaxed and think nice thoughts which the pony may well pick up! Give him a good trial; for example, ride him on both reins in all gaits on straight lines and turns, over several varied jumps if appropriate. Give him a short break on a long rein, then try again. All the time, be guided by both your advisor and your own instinct.

If you like the pony, ask about the chances of having him on trial. Provided you insure the pony fully from the moment he leaves his owner's premises, this is a reasonable request, but not all sellers will agree.

Having him vetted

Some purchasers, very unwisely, try to save money by not having the pony checked over by a veterinary surgeon (veterinarian) before buying him. It is surprising how many ponies look fine and behave well but who turn out to have heart disease, poor eyesight, lung problems or early joint problems which will sooner or later severely restrict the pony's work potential.

Sometimes a condition will be present although unlikely to affect a pony's performance, but you still need to know about it. Other conditions like so-called stable vices may affect a pony's general health and you will need to discuss this with your vet. Ponies with problems are normally considerably cheaper than perfectly healthy ones.

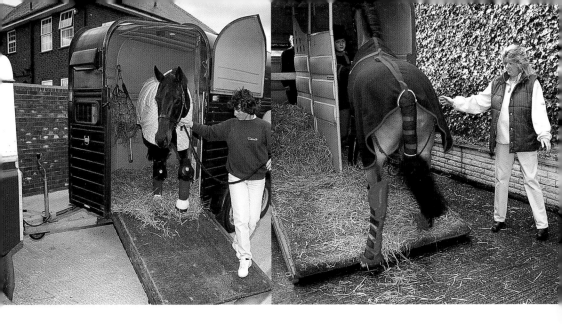

The vet will examine the pony and send you a report on his state of health on the day he examined him, also stating whether or not he should be sound (healthy) enough for the work you have in mind. There is nothing to say that the pony will remain like this for the rest of his life (he probably won't) or that he won't get some disease or other the day after. This is part of the risk of buying ponies and it is the buyer who has to take that risk. All you can do is take all reasonable precautions, be guided by your advisor and vet and trust to luck.

You will usually use a vet near to the pony's home for reasons of economy (travelling fees) but not the one who already attends the pony and who would not therefore undertake the job for reasons of ethics.

Bringing your pony home

You will have to make arrangements to transport your pony home if it is too far to ride or drive him. You are his legal owner from the time the money changes hands and he leaves his former owner's premises so you must make sure all insurances are in place.

Before his arrival, make sure his stable has been thoroughly cleaned out and disinfected with a horse-friendly disinfectant (probably one recommended by your vet), is fully bedded down with *new* bedding (so that there are no remains of a previous occupant's smell), that there is plenty of hay or haylage and fresh water waiting and there is someone to welcome him – you and your friends or family if you are keeping him at home, the yard owner or staff if he is at livery, and so on. This may sound silly but it all creates a friendly, welcoming atmosphere at a time which can be worrying for the pony. Remember, he hasn't a clue what is happening to him, where he is going or what the next few seconds hold. Friendly neighbours should be stabled next door and you should give him a tasty feed to help him settle in.

Above: *If you are having a pony on trial, you are responsible for his welfare so ensure that you have adequate insurance.*

Above right: *If the pony has to back out of his transport vehicle, make sure that there is someone on the ground to help guide him down.*

Left: *You should get a Bill of Sale or at least a receipt that proves that you now own the pony.*

Find out from his previous owner exactly what his diet has been so that you can start from there, making any changes very gradually. It is best to buy a bale of his previous hay or, if possible, haylage, from the previous owner so that you can start to mix it with your own supply and avoid sudden changes in feeding which can really upset ponies. Also, a familiar-smelling and tasting feed will, again, help him to settle.

If he is to live out or be turned out, he should be introduced to his new herdmates slowly and correctly. The worst possible thing is for him to be bundled into an existing herd, with its strictly established pecking order, because he will certainly be regarded as an intruder and almost as certainly be kicked, bitten and bullied out of the herd to lead a very lonely existence on its fringes. This sort of treatment can take a pony a very long time to get over, and is definitely not what you want for your pony.

Introducing his friends

The way to introduce a new pony into an existing herd is to choose one, friendly, low-ranking pony (ask the yard owner which one would be suitable) and request that the two of them get to know each other first, perhaps by going on a ride together or being led around together before being turned loose – just the two of them – into a paddock.

Very carefully, the others can be similarly introduced over a few days, with the most dominant ponies or horses last. This should ensure that your newcomer has at least one or two friends and is seen by the

Above: *Leading your new pony into his well prepared stable, with food and water waiting, is an exciting moment.*

Above right: *Ponies must be properly introduced to each other if you are to prevent any fighting and avoid the possibility of injury.*

others as having been accepted. There *will* be lots of squealing, bottoms up, prancing around, sniffing and snuffling – this is normal getting-to-know-you behaviour – but any serious kicking or bullying must be nipped in the bud by separating out the offenders. Any responsible livery yard owner will understand this procedure and you should check beforehand that this careful introduction period will be allowed before you sign up to a particular stable. Anyone who is difficult in this regard will probably be unco-operative in other respects, too.

TIP: *It may be advisable for ponies whose herd is being disrupted to have their hind shoes removed to minimize kick injuries, although this can be inconvenient and expensive and, therefore, may not be possible.*

If your pony is to live out, it is far safer for him to be put into his new field in daylight and for you to lead him right round the fence line before letting him loose, perhaps with his new companion, so he is certain just where the boundaries are. Although ponies can see better in the dark than humans, it is best to play safe so that you minimize the risk of your pony galloping into a fence or tree during his first night.

Most ponies, whether stabled, yarded or at grass, will feel strange at first but if you settle them in as described above you have done all you can; the rest is down to him and his new friends.

care of the
pony at grass

Many people think that because a pony is living at grass (in a field) he is living a natural life and does not need any particular care. A domestic field, however, is not at all like the many square miles of natural land a wild or feral pony would have available and ponies at grass do need care, sometimes almost as much as a stabled pony.

Winter and summer care

Ponies kept outside are particularly subject to the vagaries of the weather, and there are specific things to watch out for during the year.

Remember that in summer

◆ Ponies can suffer greatly from flies and hot sun if they have no effective shelter.

◆ They can become dangerously fat on the relatively rich grazing (compared to hills and moors) which grows in many fields, and can also develop an extremely painful foot disease called laminitis brought on by too much food (usually starches and sugars as are found in spring grass, but also by other substances). See page 156.

◆ During the grazing season (spring, summer and autumn), you must pick up your pony's droppings from the land to avoid it becoming infested with parasite eggs. All ponies have these worms, and picking up droppings which contain their eggs (even when the ponies are regularly dosed to get rid of them), helps keep the land 'clean'. It is quite a chore and has to be done several times a week.

Remember that in winter

◆ Ponies can be extremely uncomfortable if they have no shelter from driving wind, sustained rain or snow and muddy or waterlogged ground.

◆ They need extra food to keep them warm and healthy; it is wrong to think that they can exist on whatever pickings they find in a winter field.

◆ They can get a painful skin disease called mud fever if forced to exist on land which is badly poached (muddy and damaged due to ponies' hooves). A similar disease called rain rash or rain scald can occur on the upper parts of the body (top half of the neck, shoulders, back and hindquarters) in constantly wet weather.

Suitable facilities

It is much easier to keep a pony with decent facilities than to have to struggle and worry because things are not what they should be.

Always remember that your pony needs

◆ well-drained land to live on;

◆ strong, safe and secure hedges or fences and gates;

◆ a strong shelter with an open front so he can get away from extremes of weather in all seasons;

◆ enough suitable grazing;

◆ a constant supply of clean water;

◆ the company of at least one other friendly pony.

The pony has to be kept safe and secure; many of them will try to escape from whatever field you put them in! As his owner, you are legally responsible for his conduct so it pays to keep him where he can do no harm and be in no danger.

Above: *Strong, safe fences and gates are essential for safety and keeping ponies where they belong – in the paddock.*

Left: *This fencing has a strand of plain wire on the post side of the fence to help prevent ponies banging their shoulders on the posts. Ideally, the rails should be on the other side of the posts.*

Daily routines

The best way to ensure that you are doing everything you should is to have a short list of daily jobs which need attending to at different times of year.

At any time of year

Ponies must be checked to ensure that they:

◆ are healthy and content, with no diseases or injuries;
◆ have enough of the right sort of food;
◆ have enough clean water;
◆ have decent shelter.

Every day

◆ Check that the fencing and gates are strong and in good repair – and keep the gates locked if the pony is not kept on a professional yard with someone else keeping an eye on him.
◆ Check that the field shelter is strong and in good repair.
◆ Remove any litter and rubbish from the field.
◆ See that the water supply is clean and working properly.
◆ Check that ponies are not bullying each other and keeping each other from food and water.

Spring and summer

Keep an eye on the grazing and your pony's condition (see page 156). If he becomes too fat or you know that he has had laminitis previously, you may need to restrict his grazing and keep him either stabled or on a surfaced, covered area during the day (away from sun and flies).

In the morning

◆ Check that the pony is well and not being bullied.
◆ Check the fences, gates and shelter.
◆ Check the water supply.
◆ Give hay or haylage if the grass is very poor.
◆ Remove droppings from the shelter.
◆ Dandy brush the pony all over and pick out his feet, also checking his shoes (see page 94).
◆ Put on a headcollar (halter) with fly fringe and apply insect repellant all over the pony. Special safe headcollars are available for field use which will break and fall off if they become caught up. Other headcollars such as leather or cotton webbing only break after tremendous pressure and nylon web ones do not usually break at all, so are too dangerous to leave on field-kept ponies.

TIP: *Remember that ponies can become sick or injured very quickly and it is not good enough to leave them for several days, or even 24 hours, without visiting them, checking them close up (not from the field gate) to ensure they are healthy and thriving.*

In the evening

- Check that the pony is well and not being bullied.
- Check all round field again.
- Check water supply.
- Give hay/haylage if necessary.
- Remove droppings from shelter.
- Groom pony if not done in the morning, checking feet/shoes.

Autumn and winter

In the early autumn you will notice that your pony's summer coat is falling out and will soon be replaced by a longer, thicker one – this will probably be very thick if he is a native type. Ponies with Arab and Thoroughbred blood grow shorter finer coats and also have thinner skins so they cannot withstand a winter outdoors without help; you will need to rug them up.

Because of their winter coat, ponies working fairly hard (hunting, hacking, going to rallies, indoor show-jumping and so on) will probably need partly clipping (see page 132). In general, though, grass-kept ponies must be clipped as little as possible and will probably need either a very good and well-bedded-down shelter or to be brought in (yarded or stabled) at night during the colder months.

The general daily routine checks are the same as for during the spring and summer.

In the morning

- Remove the turnout rug, if worn, and check that the coat and skin are not becoming rubbed underneath it. Put it to dry and air, and either put on the dry one or leave the pony without a rug if the day is dry and mild.
- Groom, check feet and shoes. Also check to make sure that mud fever is not developing.
- Check the water supply and break the ice, if frozen, piling the ice on the other side of the fence so that the ponies do not cut themselves on it.
- Remove droppings from shelter.
- Give hay/haylage and other feed such as pony nuts or coarse mix (see pages 64–65).

In the evening

- Remove the turnout rug, check underneath it as usual and put it back on or change it.
- Groom the pony if not done in the morning: check feet, shoes and legs/belly for mud fever.
- Check water supply and break ice again, removing it from the water.
- Remove droppings from shelter.
- Give hay/haylage and other feed, as required.

Above: *Don't keep your pony at any place where there is dangerous, broken fencing.*

Left: *Picking up droppings from paddocks is a very effective way of keeping down worm infestation in your pony.*

Feeding and watering

The most important food for your pony, other than grass, is good hay or haylage. Ponies were meant to live on grass, and hay and haylage are the nearest things to it for times when grass is scarce, such as on an over-grazed paddock in summer or in winter when grass hardly grows and contains little nourishment.

Haylage is like moist hay. It is very nutritious but is fine for ponies and cobs in winter. In spring, summer and autumn, native ponies and cobs would probably be better off on hay unless there is enough grass, when they probably won't need anything else.

Many yards buy large round or square bales of haylage swathed in plastic and this can be very good. A conscientious supplier will often have an analysis of the feed value of his product, so that you have some idea of whether or not it is suitable for your pony. You can also buy smaller plastic bales of haylage with a brand name (maker's name) on them from feed merchants and some large tack stores. These will have the analysis printed in a panel on the sack.

With both haylage and hay, you can take a sample of feed along to your vet (veterinarian) and ask him to get it analysed for you: this is not being super-picky – the wrong feed can cause your pony a lot of problems.

Hay this usually is not so 'rich' or nutritious as haylage and may be a safer year-round feed for native ponies and cobs. Most hay has about 7 to 9 MJ of DE per kg (see panel, right) in it and, again, these ponies will need little other food, if anything, provided they have more or less as much as they can eat. In spring, summer and autumn, you will only need to provide hay if their grass is poor.

Concentrate feeds this is the name given to pony nuts and coarse mixes which normally contain cereal grains such as oats, barley and maize. There are many good makes of concentrates (also called 'short' feed or 'hard' feed) and most good firms make some especially for ponies and cobs.

They usually have all the information on the sack about how much to feed, or you can get booklets from the supplier. Of course, the makers want you to use their feeds but the fact is that most ponies and cobs living out, other than those crossed with hot bloods, hardly need this sort of food. The same energy levels apply as for hay and haylage and will be printed on the bag of a reputable brand.

How to feed

Hay and haylage are often fed to field-kept ponies in hayracks or haynets tied up at pony's head height inside the shelter, or tied firmly to fence posts, well spaced out to avoid bickering. Sometimes large racks on wheels are placed in a field and moved each day to prevent the ground around them becoming poached. These should have covers over the top, as rain can quickly ruin the feed.

energy content

For ponies and cobs, your haylage will need an energy content of 7 to 8 MJ (megajoules) of DE (digestible energy) per kg. This is the standard way of expressing energy content. In winter, you could feed 9 or even 10 MJ, especially to ponies with some 'hot' blood (Arab or Thoroughbred) in them, and they will need very little other feed provided you let them have as much haylage as they can eat.

The lower energy grades are best for native-type ponies and cobs. Even in winter, too much energy can cause health problems for them.

Above: *Large bales of hay or haylage are a reasonable way of providing roughage at times when grazing is scarce. Uneaten forage should be raked up to allow light through to the grass underneath so that it can grow properly.*

Concentrates are fed in buckets, bowls or mangers which hang on the fence rail, and someone should stay until each pony has finished to prevent stealing and fighting and to make sure each pony gets his ration.

When each pony has finished eating, take the buckets right out of the field to prevent accidents.

TIP: *If some ponies are being fed concentrates (cross-breds, or perhaps older ponies who need extra feed and those in hard work) and others are not, you should take them out of the field to be fed as otherwise a very dangerous situation could develop: ponies are naturally jealous over food, and someone is likely to get hurt.*

Above: *This water trough has rounded corners to help prevent injury, and the filling mechanism is covered to stop ponies interfering with it.*

Watering

Water can be provided from a supply laid on in the field from the mains supply and fed into self-filling troughs which fill up as the ponies empty them. The filling mechanism should be strongly and safely covered over to prevent ponies fiddling with it.

If water is not laid on, you will need a tap nearby and a long hosepipe so that you can fill cut-down dustbins or other containers (which must have no sharp edges or corners). This will probably only be possible in fields near to houses or other buildings.

The containers should ideally be emptied and scrubbed out with plain water weekly. Cut-down dustbins (which ponies can reach down into easily) can be rammed into large tyres and tied to fence posts with rope or binder twine: they can be moved down the fence weekly to prevent the ground round them becoming too poached.

Ponds, streams and rivers can be dangerous in winter if the ponies walk on ice and fall in. Many ponies die because of drowning or hypothermia in this way, so it could be best not to use these fields or to fence off the natural water supplies, maybe with electric fencing.

Care of skin and coat

Grass-kept ponies are usually more or less dirty and this is fine! They roll in mud which discourages skin parasites and actually keeps skin and coat in good condition; also, dried-on mud acts as a barrier against wind. However, you cannot put rugs or tack on top of dried mud otherwise your pony will be rubbed sore, so it must be removed sometimes.

A strong, natural bristle dandy brush and a plastic-toothed curry comb are the best tools for this job (see page 84 for details on grooming). Mud can only be removed once it is dry: wet mud must be left to dry and brushed off, or hosed off – and then in winter you have a soaking wet, long-coated pony who will take hours to dry before you can put on his saddle and go out for a ride. This is the reason many ponies have turnout rugs in winter!

The natural grease and dandruff in a pony's coat helps to make his coat and skin water-resistant so it should not be removed too enthusiastically; it takes a little experience, and hands-on advice from a friendly expert, to know where to draw the line between filthy and 'too clean'.

Using a body brush on a long winter coat is fairly ineffective as it cannot get through to the skin. In summer, though, this is easier and grass-kept ponies can be body brushed for special occasions like an important show. The mane and tail can be washed and your pony will look perfectly respectable.

TIP: *It's best not to shampoo grass-kept ponies. The pony needs some natural grease in his coat and, certainly in winter, he is best cleaned up by grooming.*

Above: *Some ponies love paddling and swimming, but ponds with steep sides and bottoms of deep mud are dangerous.*

Foot care and farriery

Your pony will need a visit from the farrier about once every six weeks depending on how fast his feet grow. The horn continues to grow all the time like a dog's claws or our fingernails, so the extra growth from last time will be rasped (filed) away and the feet smoothed and rounded off to their correct shape.

Finding a farrier

You will usually find a good farrier by recommendation through word of mouth from other pony-owners. Any riding school or livery yard will have a regular farrier and sometimes more than one so you should be able to find one easily. Some farriers, though, are better than others and not all of them are patient or good with ponies, so do make sure you find one who will treat your pony firmly but fairly. One bad, painful or frightening experience can make a pony bad to shoe for life – and a pony who is bad to shoe is a real liability, far from perfect!

Your farrier is the best person to decide whether or not your pony needs shoes. If the pony works mainly on soft surfaces he will not need them unless his horn is weak and soft or his feet are not naturally well-shaped. If he works on harder surfaces, does roadwork, competes or hunts, he will need shoes.

Sometimes the shoes are not worn out so the feet can be trimmed and the old shoes replaced. Usually, though, new shoes are needed.

It is your job to catch the pony up and make sure his feet and legs are at least clean, if not dry, before the farrier arrives. The farrier needs level, hard ground to work on (not the field) and somewhere to plug in his portable forge which he will bring in his van to your yard. It is also better to hold your pony, or have an adult do so if you are young, than to have him tied up for shoeing in case something startles him and he fights if tied up.

There is detailed information on shoeing on pages 94–5.

basic fitness programme
(if your pony is completely unfit)

WEEK 1: Walk out for half an hour about five days a week. Do not give both 'off' days together.

WEEK 2: Walk out for three-quarters of an hour about five days a week.

WEEK 3: Walk out for an hour about five days a week. Towards the end of this week, trot for a minute or two in the middle of the ride. Trot *steadily*, not fast, and try to keep to softish ground this week.

WEEK 4: Walk out for an hour about five days a week. By the end of the week, the pony should also be trotting steadily for two spells of two or three minutes.

WEEK 5: Walk out for an hour about five days a week. In addition, by the end of the week, the pony should also be trotting for two spells of about five minutes. Spend a minute in canter.

WEEK 6: Walk out for an hour about five days a week, plus two five-minute trot spells and about two two-minute or so in canter. This is approximate.

WEEK 7: As Week 6 but canter for two spells of about three minutes. Pony now doing up to an hour and a half exercise five days a week. Start easy jumping.

WEEK 8: As Week 7 but longer trot and canter spells, depending on how pony is going. Slightly more difficult jumping.

This approximate programme will take your pony to sufficient fitness for most tasks.

If you have problems finding ground suitable for cantering, you can do controlled canter and jumping work round a surfaced riding arena.

If you need to get the pony fitter, just continue the programme by extending the length and speed of work but do take expert advice at this point, and also check whether or not extra feeding is needed for your particular pony. Remember that every pony is different.

Above: *If you work steadily at a fitness plan for a pony, you should see the results within a matter of weeks.*

Working a grass-kept pony

One of the golden rules of feeding is that you should work your pony before feeding, not after, so that his stomach is not overloaded and pressing on his lungs, which are next to the stomach, during work. Of course, this is impossible with grass-kept ponies because they eat most of the time. You can bring your pony into a stable for an hour or so before fast work, or take consolation in the fact that grass-kept ponies eat more naturally than stabled ones and do not gorge, so their stomachs are rarely full. If you ride your pony straight from the field, make sure you walk for at least 20 minutes before doing anything energetic, and your pony should be alright.

Grass-kept ponies are often healthier than stabled ones and, surprisingly, actually fitter because they are moving about and exercising most of the time. Provided the grass is not rich, you can get them very fit. Many endurance horses and ponies live mainly at grass and have to be extremely fit.

Getting your pony fit

Getting a pony fit for work is not difficult but it takes time and many people don't bother to do it properly. Ponies who are in work most of the time remain fairly fit but those which have a longish break (of a few months) lose fitness and have to be built up again.

Feeding is said to be an important part of a fitness programme, but grass-kept ponies manage very well on their grass and steadily-increasing work other than in winter, when some concentrates will be needed.

Looking after your pony's field

Most pony-owners do not have their own land, but you need to have an idea of what should be happening to the land where your pony lives so that you can work out whether the place is well-run or not. Remember that ponies and cobs do not need very nutritious grass and can live on quite poor grass, but be guided by whether or not they look healthy. Always be ready to seek expert advice.

Ponies' grazing habits

Ponies are fussy grazers: they eat 'patchily', concentrating on the tastiest areas, allocating some areas for just doing droppings where they don't normally eat and ending up with some very short areas (called 'lawns') and some long, neglected ones (called 'roughs').

After a few weeks' grazing, a pony paddock looks very uneven with these areas of long and short grass: it is time to treat and rest it and move the ponies on. The long grass left should be grazed by sheep or cattle and any remaining after a couple of weeks cut down (called 'topping'). Then the paddock should be harrowed and rested for a few weeks till the growth has evened up and the ponies can return. Their second paddock should be treated similarly.

This system means that you need at least two paddocks so you may have to divide a larger field, maybe with removable electric fencing. Each part needs access to water and shelter.

For winter use – the driest paddock should be reserved and used as a 'throw-away' paddock because the ponies will damage it. However – and this is a point which is very hard to bring home to some landowners – in spring when the other paddocks come back into use, the winter one is topped, harrowed (scraped with a heavy metal spiky chain-like square pulled behind a tractor to air the soil and drag out dead material) and fertilized to feed it. Then it is left to rest and a couple of months later you will not know it ever had ponies on it. It can then be grazed again for three months to rest the others, then rested itself in preparation for winter use.

In spring, summer and autumn – it is warm enough for worm eggs in droppings to hatch out their larvae or young forms which ponies eat with the grass. Droppings should really be picked up from the paddocks every two days to minimize infestation. Dose your pony against worms according to your vet's (veterinarian's) advice (see page 154–5).

There is much more to land management but this gives a basic idea of how it should be treated. Sadly, some pony paddocks receive no care at all and become sour, neglected, full of weeds and useless.

Dental care

Like us, all ponies need a visit from the dentist about twice a year. A vet (veterinarian) can come and see to your pony's teeth and there are equine dentists (who, strictly speaking, should be called 'equine dental technicians') who visit yards and often do a really excellent job.

Ponies' top jaws are wider than their bottom jaws, and the jaws move in such a way as to make the outside edges of the upper back teeth and the inside edges of the lower back teeth very sharp, which can cut the cheeks and tongue. This makes it very uncomfortable for ponies to eat properly and mouth problems can also cause difficulties when being ridden.

signs of problems with teeth

The pony may chew very slowly and carefully and look uneasy.

He may make strange movements with his head when eating.

He may drop partly chewed food out of his mouth.

There may be unchewed food in his droppings, either grain or lengths of hay or grass.

He may toss his head when being ridden, start to pull or be apparently disobedient, trying to avoid the action of the bit.

He may start to lose weight because he cannot eat properly.

You should have your pony's teeth checked at least once a year and preferably twice. Old and young animals usually need checking more often. You can ring your vet (veterinarian) or a good equine dentist and he or she will come to the yard, inspect the teeth, rasp down any sharp edges, clip off any overgrown pieces and generally see that all is in order.

Your vet will have to cope with problems such as broken teeth, abscesses, bad teeth which need removing and so on, but the dentist will tell you about these.

If people tell you that there is no need to fuss about teeth, don't believe them. There is!

Below: *Square mesh fencing can be dangerous for ponies who often get their hooves and legs through fencing and injure themselves trying to get free.*

Rugs (blankets)

A couple of good, well-designed, well-fitting turnout rugs (blankets) can be a big advantage to most ponies although many owners rug up their ponies when they really should not. It can be actually cruel to put a heavy turnout rug on a native pony unless the weather is really grim – but it is also cruel to turn out a finely-bred, clipped pony on a bad winter's day without one.

Some people rug up outdoor ponies in warm weather solely to keep them clean, which is also very unkind unless it is a very lightweight sheet and there is a special show coming up.

Ponies are generally happier and healthier with their full coats on and no rugs but with access to good shelter. If you want to work your pony in winter, though, this can be inconvenient because of a long, wet, muddy coat and the fact that the pony will sweat heavily. Therefore, in winter, ponies may benefit from clipping and rugging up. Types of rug and how they should fit are explained on pages 110-11.

TIP: *If, at any time, summer or winter, you find that your pony is unhappy living at grass (usually, but not always, because there is no field shelter), you must find some decent stabling for him and stable him for at least part of his time, probably at night in winter and during the day in summer. To do otherwise and just leave him to it is cruel.*

Stabling at night – is it necessary?

It may be hard to believe that even the hardiest of our native ponies do like some shelter! When you imagine these furry, tough little ponies, you may think that their coats provide all they will need, but in their natural environment they can seek out trees, shrubbery, hills, dips in the ground and maybe rocks and cliffs to find some sort of a break from the weather. In a bare, domestic field they will have little or no real shelter and will need a proper field shed, sited with its back to the prevailing wind and on the driest part of the field.

Another good plan is to arrange their stabling so that the doors are left open and they can come in and out of the field, to and from the stabling, as they feel the need. They will be much happier and far healthier this way.

how to tell if your pony is cold

With your bare hand, feel round the base of his ears, his belly and flanks, his loins and his hindquarters. Allow several seconds for any body heat to pass through his thick coat. If he feels warm in these areas, he is fine. If he feels chilly, he needs a rug.

Have a good look at him. If he looks worried, tense and hunched up he is almost certainly cold.

If he is standing by the gate wanting to be brought in, he is probably cold and is certainly unhappy. If his fieldmates are keeping him out of the shelter, he is also miserable and probably cold.

Of course, if he is actually shivering he must be *very* cold.

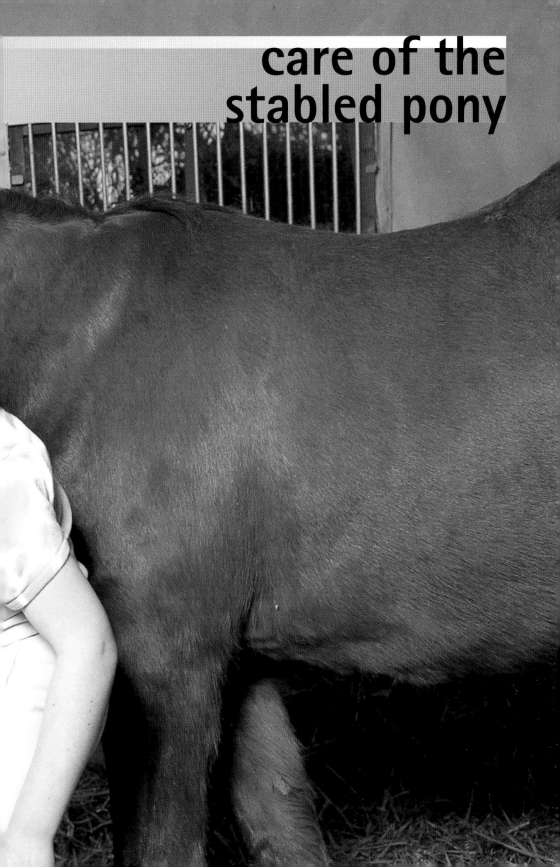

care of the
stabled pony

Although we so often see ponies in stables, and many of them spend most of their time in them, stabling is an unnatural lifestyle for them. Stabled ponies are total prisoners, but that does not mean they have to be miserable: those who are unhappy are hardly ever turned out and, to make matters worse do not have pony-friendly stables – insufficient ventilation, a poor outlook, partitions making them unable to touch and talk to neighbouring ponies, not enough clean water and insufficient hay or haylage to keep them busy and full as nature intended.

Stabling

Keeping your pony in a stable will have advantages and disadvantages for both of you.

Disadvantages

◆ From the pony's viewpoint, stabling can be restricting; he cannot do anything unless we permit it – eat, drink, exercise, play or socialize with other ponies.
◆ Some ponies will develop stable vices such as crib-biting, windsucking, weaving and box-walking.
◆ Other effects of over-confinement in unsuitable stabling include aggressiveness which is not normal for the horse family, depression, wood-chewing, head-twisting, door kicking, pawing and others.
◆ From our viewpoint, stabling is very tying and a lot of work; we have to do everything for the pony – grooming, mucking out, bedding down, feeding, watering, exercising and seeing to rugs.
◆ It is expensive to keep a pony stabled.

Advantages

◆ If the pony is well exercised and stabled in good conditions, he can be quite content. Many ponies regard their stables as somewhere sheltered and safe, where they find a comfortable bed to lie and roll on, food, water, company and something interesting going on.
◆ From our viewpoint, stabled ponies are handy when we want them, easier to keep clean and smart if that is important to us.
◆ Ponies are protected from extreme climatic conditions and, even if clipped in winter, are warm because we have rugged them up.

TIP: *Remember that long periods in the stable can eventually get to your pony; make sure that he has plenty of time turned out with his friends, playing, eating juicy grass, being part of a herd and enjoying his freedom.*

Above: *Providing hay or haylage in a tub, like this, ensures that the pony eats at a natural height, with his head down, making for comfort and good digestion.*

The combined system

Apart from yarding or being out with good shelter, probably the best system of keeping ponies from every point of view is the combined system. The pony can spend some of his 24 hours stabled and some of it in the field according to what is convenient and suitable.

The system is very flexible and the times spent in or out can be very variable. Ponies can be sick or injured and then a grass-kept animal can be brought into a stable so that he may be nursed properly back to health; in practice, most owners have both stabling and field facilities available.

Daily tasks and routine

The jobs to be done for a stabled pony are the same all year round with the exception that rugs may only be used in winter, so let's see what is involved in the time-consuming task of looking after a stabled pony.

Checking the pony

- ◆ The pony must be checked daily for general health (see page 152). This only takes a few seconds and becomes instinctive with experienced, concerned owners.
- ◆ Whenever you go into the box, particularly if the pony has been stabled for some time such as first thing in the morning, check round the bedding to see if it is unusually disturbed which could be a sign that he has been thrashing around or scraping it about which, in turn, could mean he has been feeling colicky or uncomfortable.
- ◆ Check whether there are any scrape marks on the wall which could mean he has been cast (stuck against the wall with his legs folded in such a way that he cannot get up again) and has been scrabbling about trying to get up.
- ◆ Check that his previous feed and hay have been eaten and that he has drunk some water. If you have an automatically filling waterer this is impossible: check that it is working properly and that his water is clean.
- ◆ Remove rugs and check for rubs.
- ◆ Check that there are normal amounts of droppings in the bedding.

Feeding

Ponies have been developing in nature for millions of years as outdoor, running, grazing, herd animals. They need freedom and company. Their natural food is grass and domestic ponies also eat conserved versions of grass – hay, haylage and other 'forage' feeds such as short-chopped grasses, straw and alfalfa (lucerne) which are usually sold in sacks with a brand name on them.

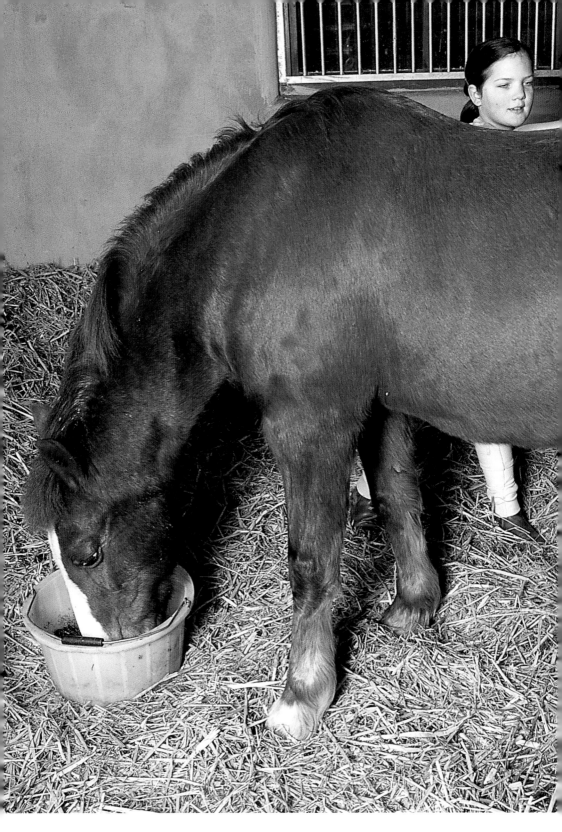

Fibre/forage feeds

The word 'forage' is used to indicate a food which is mainly fibrous in nature and which is sometimes called 'roughage' or 'bulk', such as grass, hay, haylage and chop: these sorts of feeds are excellent for ponies as their digestive systems have evolved to cope with lots of fibre but not much grain.

Short-chopped forage feeds are often called 'chaff' but this is incorrect. The correct name for hay and straw chopped up into short lengths is 'chop', for obvious reasons. The word 'chaff' really means the outside husk of grains such as oats and wheat.

Today we have chop-like feeds which are called short-chopped forage feeds and which are made variously of chopped straw, grasses and alfalfa. The branded ones are more nutritious than ordinary chop and may have vitamins and minerals added plus a light syrup which adds taste without stickiness.

TIP: *It may be best to avoid chop-type feeds with molasses in them as too much molasses makes the feed very sugary which is not good for ponies.*

All these kinds of fibrous feeds are excellent for ponies and most of them will need no other food apart from juicy 'succulents' whenever they do not have access to grass – carrots and apples, maybe soaked sugar beet pulp and perhaps turnips, swedes and fodder beets depending on availability and the pony's likes and dislikes. In general, if the energy level of the feed is correct for the pony's type and work, ponies can and should have as much fibrous feed as they can eat, as in nature, to keep their digestive systems working properly and their minds occupied.

Fibre, the material making up plant cell walls, is digested low down in the pony's digestive system and provides a 'slow-release' energy ideal for keeping him sensible during work yet with enough energy: it also provides a steady supply of warmth in cold weather so a large supply of fibrous food on a winter's night will certainly help to keep out the cold.

Concentrates

These are the grains of cereal plants (oats, barley and maize/corn, for example) and will be found in coarse mixes (sweet feeds) and ground up in cubes or nuts. We eat breakfast cereals ourselves such as muesli, porridge and cornflakes.

Ponies' digestive systems are not well designed to digest these feeds, which contain a lot of starch and are very high in energy compared with fibre. Grains contain a lot of energy concentrated into a little package, which is why cereal grains are called concentrates. They are digested higher up the digestive tract and produce quick-release energy in a sudden boost an hour or two after eating, depending on the size of the pony, which can produce silly behaviour during work or, if the pony is

Left: *It has been proved that ponies digest feed better when they eat with their heads no higher than their shoulders.*

stabled, can make him feel frustrated because he cannot get rid of the energy. Then he may do things like box-walking, kicking the walls or door, or pawing the floor.

Field-kept ponies will feel this sudden burst of warmth and energy, but it is soon over, leaving the pony feeling cold so, contrary to popular opinion, cereal concentrates are not the most effective feeds to give for warmth on a winter's night.

Concentrate feeds are most likely to be used for ponies with a good deal of Arab or Thoroughbred blood or who are working quite hard and need extra energy. With any pony, it is always best to give a good quality forage feed as the basis of his diet, only adding cubes or coarse mixes on top if he seems to need more energy for work.

There are pony cubes available with higher energy mainly from fibre sources and oils which are better for working ponies than feeds containing high amounts of cereal grains.

Reputable makers of all good feeds produce leaflets about their feeds and also print full details of how to feed them on the bag. They nearly all have helplines, too, which you can ring for free advice, so do take advantage of these if you have any queries. Your vet is obviously a good source of feeding advice and your instructor should be, too.

TIP: *Remember that most ponies and cobs do not need cereal grains and are usually safer and healthier without them. Small ponies should not have them at all, and larger ponies and cobs should only have small amounts. There are far better and safer sources of energy available.*

How to feed

Hay and haylage are often given in haynets but these must be at the correct height: your pony's head height is about right, not too high for comfort but high enough to prevent him getting his feet caught in the net if it sags lower as it empties.

A better and more natural way is to feed hay and haylage in plastic bins in a corner of the box. This way the pony is eating with his head down as in nature and he is not constantly developing the wrong muscles in his neck for riding by pulling the hay upwards and sideways out of the net.

Short chopped forage feeds can also be fed in large tubs with succulent feeds and maybe pony nuts/cubes or mixes mixed in with them.

Concentrates such as cubes and coarse mixes, if fed alone or with chop or small amounts of forage feeds, are normally fed in buckets or bowls on the floor of the box. Sometimes mangers are used, fixed in a corner of the box or hung over the door. These are often fixed too high which makes eating uncomfortable and unnatural. The top of the manger should be level with the pony's elbow and the bottom edge must be rounded off in case he stamps when eating and risks cutting his knees on a sharp edge.

Left: *It is important to keep your pony's feed and water containers well scrubbed out and rinsed daily, using fresh water.*

Golden rules of feeding

Feed little and often Ponies are 'trickle feeders' which means that they need a small amount of food passing through their digestive systems almost constantly. They have small stomachs for their size and should not be fed concentrate feeds of more than 1.3kg or 3lb at a time for a 14.2hh pony. Finely-bred, hard-working animals needing more than this should have their concentrate feeds split into two or more a day.

Water before feeding This used to be vital when ponies did not have water with them in their stables all the time. Nowadays, nearly all ponies have water available all the time so this rule has lost its significance. It was felt that drinking large amounts after feeding would wash undigested grain out of the stomach before it was sufficiently prepared for further digestion, and would cause colic.

Now we know that drinking small amounts before, during and after eating, actually improves digestion. Remember that a pony's natural food is moist, not dry, so it is normal to add a little water to bucket feeds to damp them.

Make changes in diet gradually The pony's digestive system is very sensitive and it works by means of countless microscopic organisms in the gut which digest different foods for him. Therefore, to give

Above: *Automatic drinkers are fine but most are fitted too high for small ponies. This one is low enough for small ponies to drink from comfortably. If automatic drinkers are positioned too high, ponies often make themselves short of water by drinking as little as possible.*

time for these organisms to build up in numbers to cope with a new food, it must be introduced very gradually, perhaps starting with only 0.1kg or ¼lb daily and building up over a fortnight or so to the amount needed.

Similarly, foods must be reduced gradually so as not to upset the balance of the micro-organisms in the gut.

Do no strenuous work immediately after feeding This is so that the stomach will not be pressed on by the lungs (which will be working harder and be fuller during work), interfering with digestion. Leave an hour after feeding concentrates before fast working. If your pony has been eating hay or grass, you can go for your ride provided you walk for at least 20 minutes before trotting steadily on. Ponies feeding constantly and naturally can cope safely with slow work like this.

Feed succulents daily If your pony is on grass nothing else is needed. If not, give him carrots, apples, soaked sugar beet pulp, swedes, turnips or whatever else he likes, say 0.4kg or 1kg (1 or 2lb) in each feed depending on his size.

Feed him as an individual All ponies are different so feed yours according to his type or breed, his individual constitution (whether or not he is a 'good doer' or 'easy keeper' who puts weight on easily or a 'poor doer' or 'poor keeper' who does not), according to his level of work and the weather, more food being needed in cold or wet weather. Be prepared to get expert advice when in doubt.

Feed at the same times each day Ponies and their digestive systems like to have a routine so that they know what to expect. Grass, hay, haylage and forage feeds should always be available so he eats in small amounts and never gets really hungry. Hunger is unnatural to ponies and upsets the micro-organisms in their intestines, so if you give concentrates feed at regular times, often morning and evening, or just evening.

TIP: *Ponies used to being fed at certain times become cross if you are late and start banging stable doors and injuring their legs. Field ponies gather round the gate and arguments start with the risk of injuries, so aim to be on time.*

Use only good quality feed All feed should smell sweet and wholesome and look clean and bright. Never use dusty, mouldy, sour or musty-smelling feed, or dry feeds which have become damp or gone 'off' through being kept too long. Branded feeds should have a use-by date printed on the bag. Haylage should normally be used within a few days of opening the bale.

Hay can be kept for many months away from rain. However, you should always soak even apparently good hay for five minutes to half an hour, let it drip for a while, then give it to the pony. This is because it contains some spores of fungi or natural dust which can seriously damage a pony's lungs when dry, and damping swells the particles to a size too big to be breathed into the tiny airspaces in the lungs. Do not let it dry out again after soaking as the spores will shrink again and do their damage.

Feed plenty of fibre This means grass, hay, haylage or forage feeds. These foods are easily digested by ponies and are essential to their health and comfort. Their importance has already been discussed earlier.

Weigh all feed You may feel this is unnecessary, but it is surprising how easy it is to misjudge amounts. You may think you are feeding 0.5kg (1lb) of nuts, say, whereas really you are feeding only 0.25kg (½lb) or even 1kg (2lb). Measuring feeds just by the scoopful is very hit-and-miss. Hay and haylage can be weighed in nets or opened-out sacks on a spring weigher with a hook. Even if you feed fibre all the time it is useful to know how much your pony normally eats, and if you weigh any left-over food you will know how his appetite is varying. Big differences could mean a health problem.

TIP: *It is safer to slightly underfeed ponies than to overfeed them, certainly as far as cubes and coarse mixes are concerned.*

Grooming

Grooming a stabled pony is a necessary part of his care. It is time consuming and quite hard work if you do it properly, especially if you are not fit. You need to keep the pony clean because, being under cover and often wearing rugs, his skin is not naturally cleaned by the rain. The grease and natural dandruff builds up and can cause skin irritations, disease and encourage skin parasites. Correct grooming prevents all this.

Another important benefit of grooming is that it gives you a chance to really inspect the pony closely every day and to build up a caring bond with him. Proper grooming is a form of massage and your pony will enjoy it and associate you with something which feels good.

Grooming kit
A grooming kit consists of
◆ A hoof pick for cleaning out underneath the feet.
◆ A dandy brush with fairly long, stiff bristles (natural bristle is the most effective) for removing stable stains (dried on urine and droppings), dried sweat and mud.
◆ A body brush with short, finer bristles for getting right through the coat to the skin for removing dust, dandruff and excess grease from the coat and skin.
◆ A metal curry comb with teeth and ridges for cleaning the body brush, *not* the pony.
◆ Two sponges, one for cleaning the eyes, nose and lips and another for cleaning under the dock, between the buttocks and between the hindlegs – the udder (in a mare) or sheath (in a gelding).

Optional extras include
◆ Cactus cloths or cactus mitts for cleaning ponies who dislike brushes.
◆ A water brush, like a smaller dandy brush with softer bristles, for damping and laying the hair of the forelock, mane and tail to flatten and smarten them.

- A plastic-toothed curry comb for helping to remove mud and dead winter coat in spring.
- A rubber curry comb for the same purposes.
- A rubber (like a tea towel – you can use old ones) used very slightly damp for giving the coat a final smoothing and polishing after body brushing. An old silk scarf is also excellent and puts a good shine on the coat.

How to groom

If the weather is reasonable, tie your pony up outdoors to groom him so that the air in the stable does not become full of dust.

Quartering

This is the quick tidy up given before riding. You should:

1 pick out the feet with the hoofpick into either a dustbin lid or a special shallow container or old bucket so the dirt does not fall into the bed.

2 brush off stable stains, dried sweat and mud with the dandy brush – *carefully* – so that you do not scrub at and annoy the pony but firmly enough to do the job.

3 pick all bedding out of the mane and tail and brush them with the body brush.

4 finally, damp-sponge the eyes, nostrils and lips (don't wash the sponge in the pony's drinking water!).

Full grooming

This is done on return from exercise once the pony has dried off but is still warm. His coat and skin are toned up, warm and easier to clean.

1 Pick out the feet with your hoofpick, working from heel to toe so that you do not push any grit and dirt under the loosest part of the shoe at the heels. Get right down into the grooves at the sides of the frog and into the cleft of frog in the middle. Be careful but firm. (See page 120 for handling.)

1 A basic grooming kit: body brush (left), metal curry comb (right) for cleaning the body brush, and various sponges.

2 Additional items include a stable rubber, a rubber curry, a dandy mitt, a mane comb (for trimming, not combing) and a pair of curved fetlock scissors.

3 A dandy brush is essential, also, for removing dried mud, sweat and droppings.

4 Clean the body brush after every two strokes.

5 Carefully brush out the tail a few hairs at a time. Many people don't brush manes and tails but separate the hairs with their fingers.

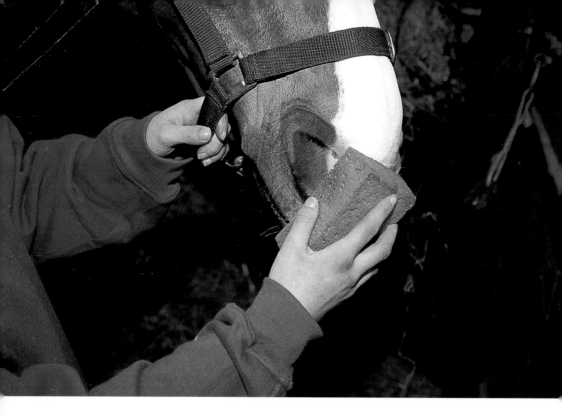

Above: *Use one sponge for the head and another for between hind legs and under tail.*

2 Use the dandy brush to remove dried mud and sweat. Don't be rough!
3 Take your body brush and put your hand through the loop on the back of it. Starting at the head, steady the head with one hand and with the other, firmly but carefully, brush in the direction of the hair with your body brush. Do the whole head, under the jaw and the ears, including brushing inside them up towards the tip. Every six strokes or so, scrape the bristles along the teeth of the metal curry comb to clean them. To knock the dandruff and powdery grease out of the curry, occasionally tap it on its side on the ground, or outside the door if you are grooming indoors.

Progress to the neck and have your body brush in one hand and your metal curry comb in the other. It's usual to start with the brush in your left hand if doing the near (left) side and vice versa, but your arm will get tired soon so it's all right to swap over – no matter what the books say! Stand with the elbow of your brush arm slightly bent and place (don't slap) the brush on the coat. Lean your bodyweight on to the brush and brush the pony in long, firm, sweeping strokes all over. This is less tiring than pushing with your arm. Be gentle over bony areas such as shoulders, withers, hips and legs, and don't forget to keep cleaning the brush with the curry comb.

4 Clean the forelock, mane and tail with your body brush, never your dandy brush. Some people only use their fingers for this task so that hair is not pulled out. Separate the forelock into locks and brush right out

from the roots where grease gathers. Throw the mane over to the other side of the neck and bring it back by brushing from the roots one lock at a time. Hold the tail at the end of the dock with all the hair in one hand and your brush in the other; then gradually let down a few hairs at a time and, starting by brushing down at the ends, gradually work up the hairs to the dock to brush out the grease, then let down another few hairs and continue like this till the whole tail has been done.

5 If you have a water brush, dip the bristle tips in water (not the drinking water) and firmly shake the brush downwards to remove excess, then brush the top layer of the forelock, mane and tail to 'lay' them.

6 Damp sponge the 'front and back ends', *keeping the sponges separate and never mixing them up*, to remove dust and discharges.

7 Give a final polish with the rubber, if you wish – and you've finished.

This will take at least half an hour if you are used to it and probably longer.

TIP: *Areas often overlooked when grooming are under forelock and mane, under jaw, between legs, belly and behind pasterns, so don't be guilty of doing only half a job!*

Above: *Remove droppings as often as you can to keep your pony's feet in good health and to keep the bedding cleaner.*

shampooing – what you'll need

Ideally, a hosepipe attached to a warm water supply. Otherwise, two or three large buckets of just-warm water (if the weather is very hot, cold water will do).

Two large sponges, one for soaping and one for rinsing if you have no hosepipe.

Special mild animal or pony shampoo.

A sweat scraper, a semi-circular blade of rubber on a metal frame and handle for squeezing water out of the coat.

Several old towels.

A clean rug or sheet to cover and dry the pony off, this should be a 'breathable' type to allow moisture to escape, and stable bandages for legs.

Top: *The items needed to shampoo a pony.*

Above: *Thoroughly lather your pony down to the skin and rinse off very thoroughly.*

Shampooing

Ponies should only be shampooed if really necessary and grass-kept ponies not at all. It should not be done on cold days.

1   Wet the pony all over but be careful, if doing the head, not to get water in eyes and ears.

2   Apply shampoo to pony or sponge and quickly lather him all over with the sponge, again keeping well away from eyes and ears. Do the mane, and wash the tail by dunking it in a bucket and lathering it, not forgetting the dock.

3   Using your hosepipe or second sponge, slosh clear water all over the pony using as much fresh water as you need to remove every last bit of lather. Don't forget to rinse under the mane and forelock, under the belly, between the legs, behind the pasterns and under the tail, where soap may remain. Dunk the tail in clear water and rinse the dock, then hold the dock at the end and whirl the long tail hairs round in an upright circle to get the water out.

4   Using your sweat scraper, or the edges of your hands if you don't have one, wipe all over the pony's body to get the water out.

5   Rub him all over firmly but not roughly to partly dry him off.

6   Put on rug/sheet and leg bandages unless it is a warm day, and lead him round to keep him warm and dry off. Put on his normal rug, if worn, and leave him with hay and water. The first thing he will probably do is roll but this is normal and makes him feel better so do not stop him.

Mucking out and bedding down

This is one of the most time-consuming jobs in pony care, if it is done properly, and a very important one. Ponies do not like living among their own urine and droppings: they do not do so in a field where they allocate particular areas as loos, but in a stable they have no choice.

The three main reasons for mucking out are:
- It is pleasanter for the pony to live in hygienic surroundings;
- Dirty bedding gives off gases and harbours dust and fungi which harm his lungs;
- Dirty bedding causes foot infections commonly known as thrush which can be very hard to cure once established and can even make the pony lame.

Different bedding materials

The two main bedding materials used now are shavings and wheat straw. Straw, like hay, is prone to carrying fungal spores which can cause allergic reactions and lung disease in some ponies, even the short-chopped, medicated sort because the fungi tend to be in the middle of the stalks where the disinfectant does not reach. Wood shavings are normally healthier but can be very dusty, so buy the cleaned sort usually described as 'dust extracted'.

The object of mucking out is to remove droppings and urine-soaked bedding from the stable, leaving behind older clean material and adding new as needed. There are three systems, with various personal compromises, but so long as the air in your pony's stable is fresh and his bedding is mainly clean, you should have no health problems.

The three systems are:
- Full mucking out in which you remove all the droppings and dirty bedding daily and wash down the whole stable floor, disinfecting it daily. This is the most hygienic system.
- Semi-deep litter in which you remove all the droppings and the worst of the bedding daily, rake old, clean material into the middle from the sides and add new bedding as needed. This method is quite reasonable in well-ventilated stables and provided a full muck-out is done once a week.
- Full deep-litter in which you only remove the droppings several times a day, ideally, and lay ample clean bedding on top of the dirty bedding. This system really only works in covered yards and stables which have most of their top halves open or have many ventilation

avoid rubber matting

Rubber matting is sometimes used as flooring in stables. This is most unpleasant for ponies, who are left without bedding all day. In natural conditions, ponies can stale (pass urine) on to an absorbent, soft surface: on rubber matting, they splash themselves, which they hate so much that many will put off staling until they are absolutely forced to – hardly considerate pony management.

If you do use rubber matting for warmth and cushioning, put some bedding on top.

Left: *Mucking out completely is hard work but is by far the most hygienic method. If you're fit, it should take you about half an hour.*

points. The base builds up in due course and is a Herculean task to remove manually, which is necessary if you cannot fit a mechanical digger through the door!

Full mucking out is usually only done with long straw: chopped straw and shavings are more time consuming to do because they are so bitty, but it is possible.

Full mucking out

Once you know how to do this you can compromise and manage any bed.

1 Remove all obvious droppings with a shovel into wheelbarrow or sack. Some people use strong rubber gloves and their hands for this.
2 Place all clean material in one corner of the box, using a different corner each day so that each side will be swept every few days.
3 Shovel or fork out all dirty, wet bedding into the barrow or sack.
4 Hose or swill down the floor and scrub well with the broom, sweeping all water and debris out of the door to a drain hole which may be in a corner at floor level on the wall. Lightly disinfect at this point, if desired.
5 Ideally, leave the floor to dry and air whilst the pony is out.

Bedding down – you should:

1 Take any semi-dirty material which is not too bad and lay it evenly on the floor.
2 Make another layer on top of this with old, clean material saved from mucking out.
3 Finally lay a top layer of new material on top.
4 Many people now like to make banks of further new bedding round the sides of the stable in the belief that they make the stable warmer and

Tools needed for mucking out

Wheelbarrow or muck sack

Shovel

Shavings rake, or four-pronged fork for straw

Stiff yard brush, bristle being best as plastic bristles split and clog up with bedding protect the pony, also making it difficult for him to become cast as the banks are supposed to 'bounce' him back into the centre of the floor. The trouble is that many people hardly ever remove these and clean underneath them: they become hot-beds of disease, harbouring dust, decaying bedding and droppings in which fungi and bacteria thrive. This is most common with shavings. If you do have banks, don't leave them down indefinitely. They should really be removed and redone weekly, probably at weekends when you can do a full shavings muck-out.

Muck disposal

Many yards put their muck straight into strong plastic sacks and leave them at the yard gate on the roadside where they are usually eagerly taken away as free fertilizer by gardeners. Some make a small charge per bag, and ask for the bags to be returned.

Below: *Sweep the floor thoroughly: use the back of your shovel blade to scrape off stubborn dirt.*

Larger yards usually arrange for a contractor such as a nursery or market garden to come and remove their muck weekly.

If you keep your muck for use on your own land, it must be *at least* a year old before you put it down to ensure there are no viable worm eggs left, so you will usually need space for three muck heaps – one old and ready for spreading, one in the process of rotting and your current one.

Muck heaps should be sited downwind of stables to avoid smells and be near a gateway or drive to allow access for vehicles coming to remove them.

Exercising

Stabled ponies' exercise can include being ridden or led out in-hand (at halter), long-reined (long-lining) or lunged. Ridden exercise is the most effective but ponies also enjoy being led out or long-reined around the lanes and, also, lungeing if done properly (steadily and on large circles or ovals) for limited periods. To lead out and long-rein, you obviously need to be fairly fit and agile to keep up with the pony's natural gait and have good control.

It is said that a stabled pony needs about two hours exercise a day if he cannot be turned out but this is minimal; being indoors for 22 hours out of 24 is too long. Try to get your pony out and about as much as possible, with expert help if necessary.

Riding on the road

◆ Make sure you wear reflective/fluorescent riding clothes which are widely available now, and put reflective strips on your pony's legs to attract motorists' attention.

◆ Make sure you know and follow the rules of the road, are a good rider and have excellent control of your well-shod, well-behaved, traffic-proof pony.

◆ It is always safer to ride out in company than alone.

◆ Ideally, one member of the party should have a first-aid qualification.

TIP: *Always wear your hard hat, never go out in fog and always use a light if you absolutely have to ride or lead in the dark.*

Using riding tracks

◆ Treat the countryside and its work considerately.

◆ Do not canter through crops or fields of other animals. Leave gates as you find them, open or closed.

◆ Be polite to people you meet.

◆ If anyone treats you badly report it to the police and to your local Pony Club (4H Club) or riding club official.

◆ *Keep to the tracks* and if you find any blocked report them to your local authority.

Above: *A good way to stabilize water buckets is to stand them inside a close-fitting car tyre.*

An exercise routine

◆ Have your identification in a pocket and the pony's on a disk on his saddle so you can both be traced should you have an accident.

◆ Have a simple first-aid kit in your pocket – lint or Gamgee Tissue for padding over a wound, a large coin to apply pressure to stop bleeding, and a bandage. You can use these on people or ponies.

◆ Have money for the phone or a mobile phone with you.

◆ Always walk the first 20 minutes out and the last 20 minutes home to warm your pony up and then to cool him down.

◆ Although you want to enjoy your hack, keep your wits about you and do not slop along on a loose rein particularly if there are traffic, animals or other people about. A long rein is fine for relaxation but keep a light contact.

◆ Trot no faster than a steady, 'working' trot on hard surfaces and walk on very soft or rough ground; if you can't avoid this type of ground, keep a light contact and let the pony pick his own way. If you cannot avoid ice, quit your stirrups, keep a light contact and sit very still and upright, trusting your pony to get you out of it.

◆ Choose cantering surfaces carefully (turf is best) to avoid jarring your pony.

♦ On return, remove tack (see page 112), let the pony have a drink and a roll and brush him over or groom if dry, checking for wounds or scrapes and checking that a shoe has not become loose. Put on a breathable rug if wet. Give hay or haylage and maybe feed. Leave the pony comfortable and check him later, as normal, or get an experienced person to do so.

Foot care and farriery

We have already covered daily care of the feet and the reason for shoeing.

The shoeing process

Below: Shoeing can be a slightly uncomfortable, boring process so a co-operative, patient pony will keep your farrier in a good mood!

Your pony can be shod 'hot' or 'cold'. Most farriers today have portable gas forges which they bring to your yard in a van, with all their equipment and shoes of different types and sizes so cold shoeing is not as common as formerly.

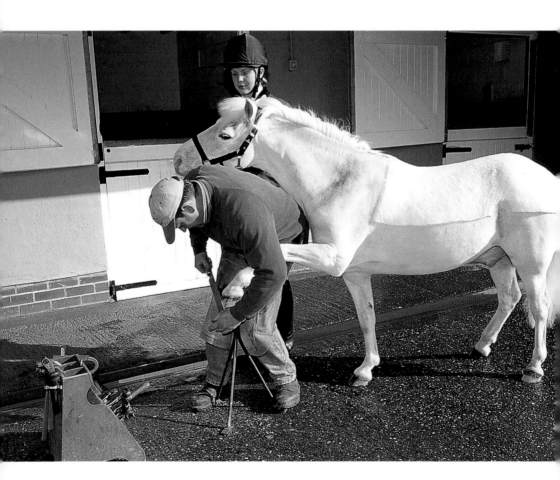

Tell your farrier what work your pony does and take his advice as to the best type of shoe for him. He may first want to see your pony led at walk and trot to study his way of going. He will check how he wears his shoes, then he will remove them and study his bare feet. Excess horn growth will be clipped and rasped off and the feet 'dressed' (trimmed to a correct shape and rounded neatly off).

The farrier will check the size of shoe your pony takes and, if shoeing hot, will heat the shoe in his forge, hammering it to fit on his anvil. He will make ('draw') clips to help keep the shoe in place on the foot: these fit into little 'cut-outs' the farrier makes in the horn. There is usually one at the toe of a front foot and two, one at each side, on a hind foot.

He will carry the hot shoe to the pony on a metal stick called a pritchel, placed in one of the holes, and will hold the hot metal against the ground (bearing) surface of the pony's foot. This should not be done for any longer than necessary and very few ponies object as they cannot feel it. They usually object to the hiss and smoke, if anything. The farrier will make any further corrections to the shape, maybe try the shoe again, then cool it down by plunging it in a bucket of cold water.

Then he will nail the shoe to the foot, trying to get the nails to come out up the wall at the same height. He will twist the ends of the nails off so that short lengths called 'clenches' are left. These he hammers down into a little groove he has made, so that they act as grippers to keep the shoe on.

Finally with the rasp he will smooth the nailed-down clenches and round the hoof where it meets the shoe and the job is done. He should then see the pony trotted up (led at trot in-hand/at halter) to make sure he is going well and is not lame, perhaps due to a nail being a little close to the sensitive structures inside the foot.

Your job now is to pay the farrier and book him again for six weeks' time to make sure he is available. If your pony damages (twists or 'spreads') or loses a shoe, or one becomes loose which you can hear from the clanking noise it makes, you can ring him and most farriers will come out to put things right.

If your pony's shoes get very worn or are left on too long, the foot may grow over the edges of the shoes, the shoes may dig into the foot at the heels and the clenches will rise from their hammered-down position. The farrier must then be called to renew the shoes (they should not be allowed to get into this state) as riding with worn shoes can be just as dangerous as riding with loose or damaged ones.

TIP: *Do not ride a pony with a loose or spread shoe. It is also not good to ride one with a shoe missing as he will feel unbalanced and will probably not go properly.*

to check if a shoe is loose

You will hear a clanking noise when the pony goes on a hard surface, instead of the firm 'clip-clop' noise of the other three.

Take your hoof pick and see if you can fit its point under the shoe at the heel and move it: if you can, the shoe is certainly loose.

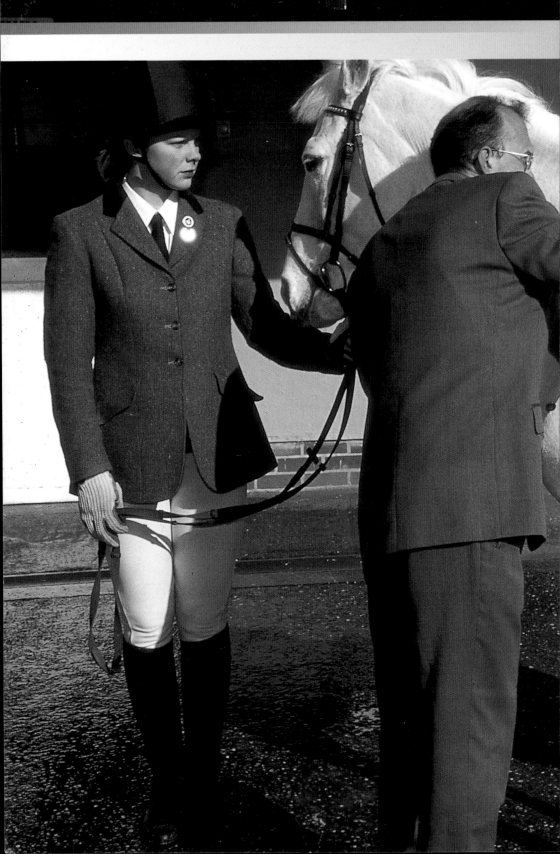

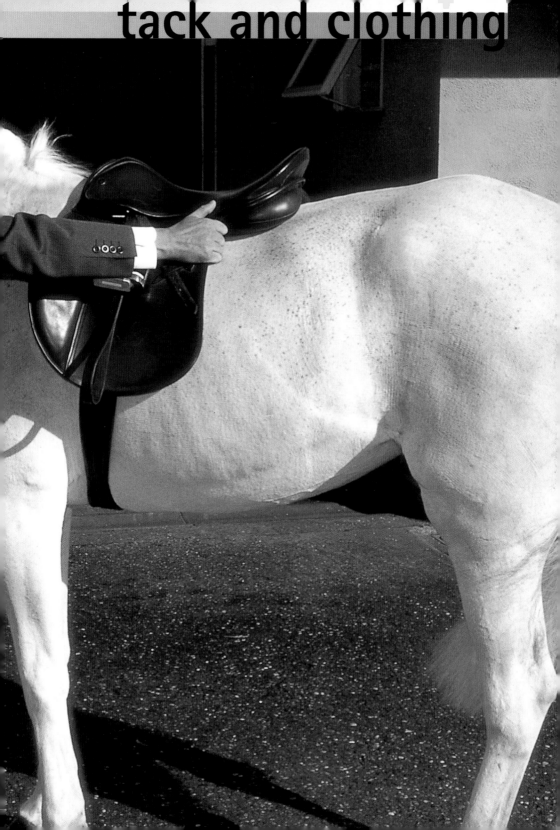

You can easily spend as much and more on tack and clothing as on your pony himself, and there is a huge selection on the market now. Don't panic when you look through mail order catalogues or round tack stores; you actually only need a fraction of the equipment you will see.

Sorting out the right tack, learning how to fit and use it and how to look after it can be very complicated, so get advice from teachers, yard owners, good tack shops and from other experienced and friendly pony owners. If you look after your tack properly it will last a long time, and will save you money in the long run.

What you really need

- ◆ A saddle is a good idea!
- ◆ A bridle with bit and reins (sold separately).
- ◆ A headcollar and leadrope for tying up and leading your pony.
- ◆ Maybe two stable rugs (blankets) if the pony is quite finely bred or will be clipped and working in winter, so that you have a spare whilst one is being cleaned.
- ◆ Perhaps a turnout rug (also called a New Zealand rug, although these are actually of a special design) if your stabled, clipped pony is to be turned out in winter, or your pony will live out, in which case you will need two. Full native ponies and cobs, though, should not need rugs if they are not clipped.
- ◆ Grooming kit, yard equipment if you have your own place, feed bins, buckets, manger and first aid kit (see page 152).

Saddles

A saddle design called a General Purpose saddle is useful for almost every kind of non-specialized riding such as hacking, cross-country work and basic dressage and show-jumping. The better ones are also suitable for endurance riding.

Whether you buy your saddle with the pony or buy it separately, and whether it is new or used, you *must* have it checked and fitted by a *qualified saddle fitter*. This is not the same as a qualified saddler or saddle maker. Saddle fitting is a skilled job and you may have to hunt around for a qualified fitter (not all tack shops employ them) but it is well worthwhile for peace of mind.

TIP: *A badly fitting saddle can damage your pony and cause all kinds of problems; make sure you get it properly fitted by an expert saddle fitter.*

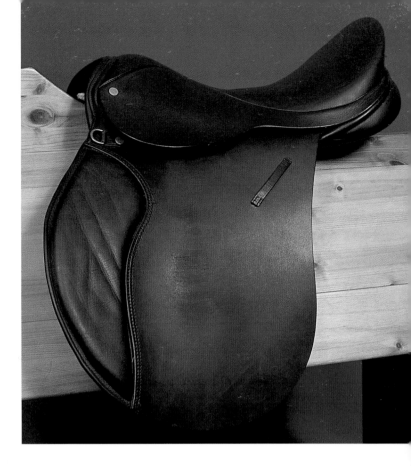

What to look for when fitting a saddle

- The saddle must sit evenly on the pony's back both from side to side and from front to back. It must be at least the width of the edge of your hand behind the top of the shoulder blades at the withers in front, and no further back than your pony's last rib (which you can feel on his side).
- Check that you can see a clear tunnel of daylight right down the pony's back from the front arch (the pommel) to the back arch (the cantle) when the pony's heaviest rider is in the saddle. This groove under the seat of the saddle is called the gullet.
- When the saddle is off the pony, check that you can fit three or four fingers' width across the gullet all the way down. The pads on either side which rest on the pony's back must be at least one hand's width, to provide a comfortable 'bearing surface' and so spread the pressure of your weight on his back.
- Never get a saddle that is so narrow that it perches above the pony's back and pinches him behind the withers, nor so wide that it rocks from side to side or even drops down and presses on the withers or spine. You should be able to fit three fingers' width between the underneath of the pommel and the top of the withers when the pony's heaviest rider is leaning forwards in the saddle.

Above: *Your saddle should not be stored on a holder that presses up inside the gullet to the underneath of the seat, as this will eventually push the saddle out of shape. A holder shaped like an upside-down V, or a seat-shaped rack are better.*

Left: *An immaculate tack room. Although tack must be kept in good order, you may be too busy looking after the pony himself to keep your tack room quite as neat.*

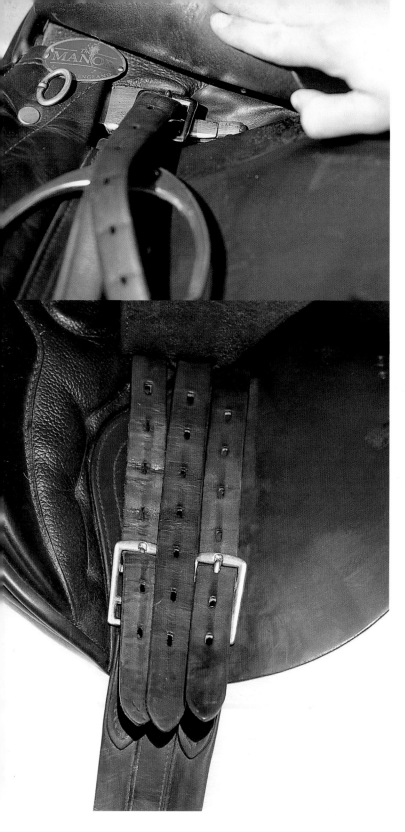

Above left: *The stirrup bar has a little catch on the end of it, the 'safety catch' which is normally kept in the down (horizontal) position, like this, so that the stirrup leather will slide off it easily in a fall.*

Left: *The customary way to fasten the girth straps is to the two outer ones: this keeps the saddle more stable and well balanced, provided the pony has good conformation and the saddle fits properly.*

Above right: *Check the tightness of your girth from the saddle by leaning down and sliding the flat of your fingers under the girth. You should just be able to fit in your fingers.*

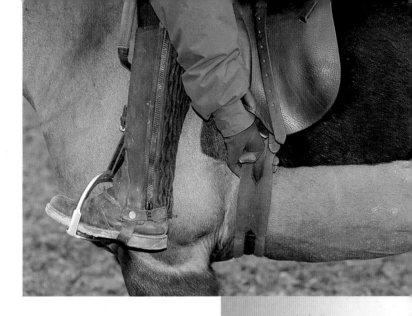

There are other more subtle aspects to fitting a saddle which are best checked by a very experienced person or a saddle fitter. Any uneven pressure or rubbing on the back can badly injure the pony and cause lameness.

Numnahs and saddle cloths

Numnahs are saddle-shaped cloths of various materials which go under the saddle, and saddle cloths are square-shaped ones which do the same. The choice of which to use is up to you. They are kept on by straps which go round the tops of the saddle's girth straps under the flaps, either by means of stitched loops or Velcro fastenings, and by loops on the bottom edge which the girth passes through.

You must always make sure that they are pulled well up into the saddle gullet so that the saddle does not press them down hard on the withers, and that they are large enough so that the seams on the edges do not come under any part of the saddle and become pressed down into the pony's skin, causing sores to develop.

Girths

The girth must be comfortable, or it can injure the pony and put him out of work. There are natural fabrics such as leather (the most common and useful) and many synthetic fabrics, too. Some are cut away or shaped behind the elbow to allow for freedom of movement (called Atherstone or Balding girths) and some have elastic to make the pony more comfortable. Girths with elastic at both ends, not just one, are best, as otherwise every time the pony breathes in, the elastic end (usually fastened on the left side of the saddle) will stretch but the other end obviously will not, giving an uncomfortable twisting feeling and moving the saddle sideways. Girths with a single insert in the middle are alright. The important point is to make sure that the girth is smooth and soft.

synthetic or leather?

There are now many children's saddles in synthetic materials and these are economical and quite acceptable. They are easy to clean (a rub down with a damp sponge is usually all they need) and as comfortable as leather. Leather ones are more expensive but last a lot longer if well cared for. The points about fit apply to both.

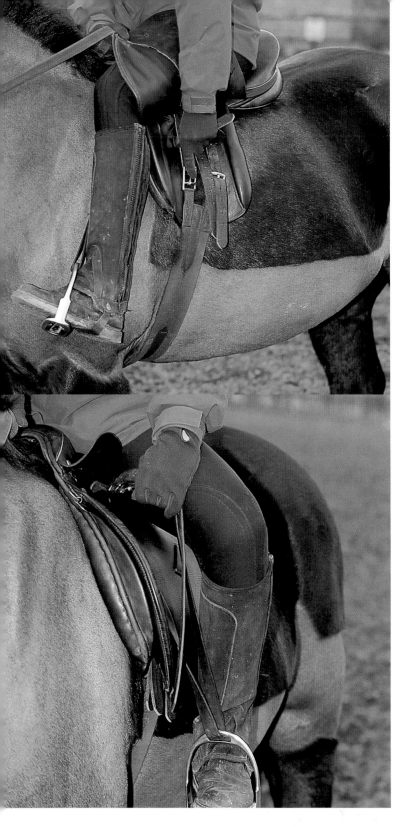

Above left: *To tighten your girth from the saddle, bring your leg forward, lift the saddle flap and tighten it one hole at a time. It should be tight enough to keep the saddle in place for safety, but not so tight that it interferes with the expansion of the pony's ribcage and so with his breathing.*

Left: *To adjust your stirrup leathers from the saddle, put your leg back a little and take the weight off the stirrup. Once adjusted, pull down on the part of the leather touching the saddle flap to bring the buckle right up to the stirrup bar, then push down with your foot.*

Right: *If the bottom (the tread) of your stirrup is level with your ankle bone when your leg is hanging down loose, your stirrups are almost certainly the correct length for you.*

Stirrups

Make sure you buy some kind of safety stirrup. There are makes in which the outer branch of the stirrup springs outward on pressure, to free your foot in a fall. Some have an outer branch curved forwards at the bottom so that your foot comes free easily, and others have a rubber loop instead of a metal branch which flies off its hook if you put pressure on it in a fall. Avoid this type because it tends to bend out of shape after a while as it has no outer branch to support it.

The inside of the bottom of the stirrup (the tread) should be 2.5cm or 1in wider than the sole of your boot at its widest part. If narrower than this your foot could be jammed in it in a fall and you could be dragged by the pony which can kill you; if it is wider, your foot could actually slip through the stirrup and you could be dragged by the ankle. You can see how important it is to have the right equipment.

Stirrup leathers

These can be synthetic (usually very strong nylon) or leather (the strongest being rawhide which are sold as unbreakable and, therefore, very safe provided you ensure that the stitching is always in good order). If the leathers are too narrow or too wide they will feel uncomfortable and look odd.

You need a width which just runs easily through the eye on the top of your stirrup. If your stirrup is the right size for your foot, the leathers will turn out to be the right width, so you can check this in the shop when you are buying them.

Above: *This safety stirrup has a forward bend on the outer branch, making it easier for the foot to be released in a fall.*

neckstrap

It's a good idea for novice riders to use a neckstrap with the saddle, providing something to hold on to if you need to keep your balance; it is very bad to cling on to the reins for this purpose. The strap, usually made of leather, goes round the bottom of the pony's neck so that you can fit the width of your hand between it and the pony, and has a leather loop at each side near the top which buckles to the front metal dees of your saddle.

Below: *Hang up your bridle on a rounded bracket so that the headpiece will stay in shape.*

2   3   4

1 Hold the cheekpieces in one hand, steadying the pony's head with that hand, and hold the bit in the other.

2 Once the pony has accepted the bit, bring the headpiece up over his ears.

3 Make the hair comfortable under the headpiece and adjust the browband so that it is comfortable, too, then fasten the noseband and finally the throatlatch.

4 This bridle fits well, the throatlatch should be looser and therefore lower.

Bridles

Bridles are available in synthetic materials which are easy to care for and good enough for everyday and use some endurance riders use them in competition, but most owners still have leather bridles.

Bridles come basically in Pony, Cob and Full (horse) sizes and sometimes in Small Pony sizes. If you tell a saddler the height of your pony, but also measure the pony's head from the corner of his mouth, up over his poll behind the ears and down to the corner of his mouth on the other side, he will know what size to offer you.

TIP: *A tasteful bridle really sets off a pony and looks very impressive whereas a cheap or flashy one will not show him to best advantage.*

What to look for when fitting a bridle

◆ The browband (which goes under the forelock below the ears) must be long enough not to pull the headpiece (which goes over the head behind the ears) forward into the base of the ears which can be very uncomfortable and can cause head tossing and 'bad' behaviour. You must be able to slide a finger easily under the browband all the way along.

◆ The throatlatch (pronounced 'throatlash') should fall half way down the rounded lower jawbones, and you should be able to fit the width of your hand between it and the jawbone. It fastens on the near (left) side.

◆ The noseband, whatever sort you use, should *not* be tight: you should be able to slide your finger easily under it all around the pony's head. It should be low enough not to rub the sharp facial bones but high enough not to come near the nostrils and interfere with breathing.

◆ The bit should *lightly* press up into the corners of the mouth so that it creates just *one* wrinkle there. Most people fit bits too high which stretches the skin, is uncomfortable for the pony and can even cause the skin to split.

Bits

There are hundreds of different bits available, but for a novice rider or inexperienced child's pony the best type is a snaffle, which has a single mouthpiece and rings on its ends to which the reins fasten.

There are many different snaffles, but for a well-behaved pony, probably the best type is a French link snaffle. This has a flat plate in the middle linked to the two branches of the bit, forming a comfortable curved shape which is also movable so the pony can play with it and move it around in his mouth. It is better than a single-jointed bit which can squeeze the pony's mouth, press into the roof of the mouth if too big, and hurt him.

The rings of the bit can either run through holes in the end of each branch, or can pass through an oval extension of the branches which is called an eggbutt ('egg' being its approximate shape, and 'butt' meaning end – so, an egg-shaped end).

With the first, loose ring type, the holes can become worn and pinch the pony's lips between the ring in the hole; this can also happen if the bit is too narrow. With the eggbutt, this cannot happen. You will need a loose ring bit, though, if your pony needs to be encouraged to play with the bit and keep his mouth moist and sensitive.

Eggbutts are best for ponies who play with the bit (called 'mouthing') too much and need a steadier feel. Your instructor will advise you on this for your own pony.

Bits are made from various materials, some said to have an attractive taste and some, usually with copper in them, said to encourage the pony to produce saliva and keep his mouth wet. Many ponies hate the taste of copper, rubber and plastic, and it is safest to use plain stainless steel which has no taste. Whatever kind you get, the mouthpiece must be very smooth and comfortable.

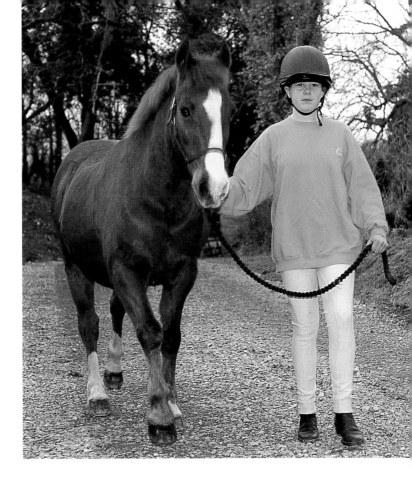

Above right: *When leading a pony in a bridle, bring the reins over his head and use them together like a rope. Whether you are using a bridle or a headcollar, always hold up the spare end of rope to prevent you or the pony treading on it and causing an accident.*

Left, top: *A mullen-mouthed or half-moon pelham bit.*

Left, middle: *A French link, loose-ring snaffle.*

Left, bottom: *A single-jointed, eggbutt snaffle.*

TIP: *You should be able to fit the width of one finger between the bit ring and the corner of the pony's mouth; if it is too narrow it will pinch, and if it is too wide it will slide about.*

Reins
There are several different sorts of reins:
◆ Plain leather which can be slippery when wet from sweat or rain.
◆ Ones with little loops of leather stitched through plain leather reins in a V-pattern or straight across which makes them easier to grip (laced leather reins).
◆ Reins which are rubber covered on either both sides or only on the side nearest the pony's neck.
◆ Synthetic reins of various sorts.

Again, take the advice of your teacher but also get what you are comfortable with.

The width of the reins is important. Children are most comfortable with reins of about 13mm (½in) wide, and teenagers and adults with small hands who may ride ponies need about 17mm (⅝in).

Left: *This headcollar is either fitted too tightly for its wearer or it is a size too small. The throatlatch should be lower on the round jawbones and the noseband should allow room for the pony to move his jaws to eat. It should also be a good two fingers' width below the sharp facial bones, not rubbing up against them, as here.*

Far right: *It is considered safer to fasten the leadrope with the fastening facing away from the pony's head.*

Below right: *Synthetic brushing boots are cheap and readily available. They are a good idea for jumping, fast work and lungeing, in particular, or for ponies who move their legs rather close together.*

Headcollars (halters)

A headcollar looks like a heavyweight, all-in-one bridle with no bit and, usually, no browband, and we discussed the safest types to get on page 62.

Most headcollars can only be adjusted by the buckle on the head-piece on the left side. Some also adjust at the nose, which is better. The best have browbands which stop the headpiece slipping down the neck and creating an uncomfortable pull on neck and nose.

The headcollar should fit so that the noseband comes two fingers' width below the sharp face bones otherwise it will rub and cause sores. The noseband is often dangerously loose and a pony could get his hind hoof in it when scratching his head with his hoof. You should be able to fit the width of three fingers between the noseband and the nose for safety while leaving enough room for the pony to move his jaws and eat.

Generally, it's not necessary to leave headcollars on ponies all the time as it can be uncomfortable for them and also dangerous: there is no need to put a headcollar on your pony unless he is being tied up or led.

TIP: *If your pony is hard to catch, put a fieldsafe headcollar on him, with a length of binder twine about 15cm or 6in long tied to the ring below his jaw (it must not be long enough for him to tread on) so that you can catch hold of him more easily.*

Boots

If your pony is inclined to kick himself (called 'interfering' or 'brushing') or if he jumps or is lunged, he will need protective boots for his legs. There are various sorts, but all have reinforced pads which go on the part of the leg to be protected. Brushing boots, the most commonly needed and used, have padded shields which fit down the inner side of the leg and fetlock and can be for front or hind legs, the latter being slightly longer. They are mainly synthetic with clip or Velcro fastenings.

You might need over-reach boots (bell boots) for jumping and lungeing. These are like upside-down bells and come in rubber or synthetic materials. Get the type with a fastening so you can put them on easily, not the sort which you have to stretch and heave over the hoof. The narrow 'neck' of the boot goes round the pastern and the bell part covers the hoof. Make sure, though, that they are only just long enough to cover the heels at the back as if they are too long they are very irritating to the pony and can interfere with his action as they flop about.

You can get special boots for travelling, too, which cover the legs from knee or hock right down to the coronet.

leadropes

Leadropes for safe leading and tying up should be no less than 2m or 6ft. Today most are made of cotton rope but there are some good synthetic ones around; just take care as nylon can be slippery. They have either a spring clip or a trigger clip on the headcollar end.

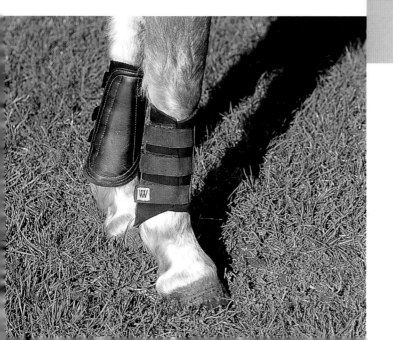

Bandages

You can get elasticated work or exercise bandages which are tricky to put on (have a lesson from your instructor and then practise) and go over felt or Gamgee Tissue padding. Stable bandages can also be used, again over padding. These are wider and longer than exercise bandages to allow for the fact that they go over the fetlock. Again, they are tricky for a novice to put on.

You may find a tail bandage is needed when you travel to stop the pony rubbing his tail. These are elasticated and very like exercise bandages, but are not put on over padding.

TIP: *Don't bandage your pony's tail too tightly, or you can injure it – it's good to have a practice and get a more experienced person to check your handiwork.*

Rugs (blankets) for indoors and out

Stable rugs

Nearly all rugs are made of synthetic materials these days. You can get thick, quilted stable rugs, thinner, thermal ones, and very light sheets just for keeping the dust off stabled ponies. It is very unlikely that unclipped native ponies and cobs will need rugs. Finer bred and clipped animals, however, will need a rug of some sort depending on the extent of their clip.

TIP: *Always check on whether or not your pony is cold before rugging him up (see page 115) as over-rugging is very uncomfortable for him.*

How a stable rug should fit

Stable rugs come with fastenings (clips or buckles) at the breast and most have crossing surcingles ('belts') passing from the off (right) side, under the belly and slotting into fasteners on the near (left) side.

◆ The front surcingle on the off side passes under the belly and goes to the back fastener on the left side, and the back surcingle on the off side also passes under the belly and goes to the front fastener on the near side.

◆ You should be able to fit the width of your hand between the surcingles and the pony – no more and no less.

◆ The front neckline of the rug should come well up round the base of the pony's neck and *in front* of the withers, never down on the points of the shoulders and back on the withers, rubbing both areas which is a common fault.

◆ The back edge of the rug should be on the root of the tail, not half way up the hindquarters.

◆ There should be no pulling on the points of the shoulders, the withers or the hips, shown by creases radiating out from these areas.

- You should be able to slide the flat of your hand easily all around between the rug and the pony at the neckline, which should be neither loose nor tight.
- Remember that the pony needs to be able to get up and down comfortably and will root in his bedding with his head down, so the correct adjustment is very important.
- When you remove the rug, if any areas show rubbed hair or bald patches, the rug does not fit properly.

Turnout rugs

Sometimes called New Zealand rugs, these are a comfort to clipped or finely bred ponies who spend time in the field. They are windproof and waterproof and are mainly made of synthetic fabrics.

How a turnout rug should fit

Turnout rugs fasten at the breast and usually have leg straps instead of belly surcingles.
- Take the left strap, make sure it is not twisted and pass it out behind and between the hind legs and clip it to its ring on the left back edge of the rug.
- Take the right strap, make sure again that it is not twisted and pass it out between the hind legs, linking it through the left strap so that they hold each other away from the sensitive skin inside the hind legs, then clip the right strap to its ring on the right back edge of the rug.
- You should be able to fit the width of your hand between the straps and the pony's thighs and this fitting is crucial.
- Tight straps are very uncomfortable and could cause the pony to gallop about trying to get away from the discomfort.
- Loose straps are a common cause of a pony getting two legs inside one strap, usually when playing and rolling; he could even break a leg struggling to free himself.

Rugs for work

These are called exercise sheets or quarter sheets (because they cover the hindquarters). They are useful for fine-skinned or clipped ponies out exercising on cold, windy days; there are cosy natural woollen ones, synthetic ones made of some sort of rain-resistant but breathable fabric, and waterproof versions called rain-sheets for when it is wet but not cold.

Exercise sheets fit under the saddle and are just like a rug with no front and no surcingles or leg straps: instead, they have loops on the bottom edge for the girth to pass through and keep them forward, plus a braided cord called a fillet string on the back edge which passes behind the thighs under the tail to stop the sheet blowing up and terrifying the pony. Like numnahs, they must be pulled well up into the saddle gullet all the way along.

Above: *This pony has a well-fitting stable rug.*

Below: *The finer bred, clipped pony on the left gets comfort from his turnout rug while his woolly friend on the right does not need a rug. It is not a good idea to leave headcollars on turned-out horses or ponies.*

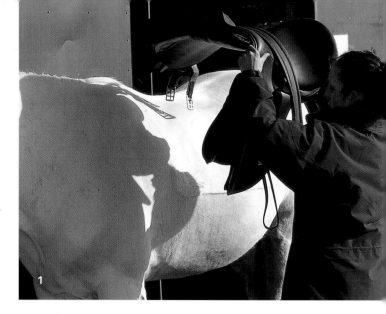

1 *Lift the saddle up and place it gently well forward on your pony's back.*

2 *Slide the saddle back well behind the withers and top of the shoulder blades to a position where it should sit comfortably on its own.*

3 *Lengthen the girth on the off (right) side so that you can girth up comfortably from the near (left) side.*

How to tack up and untack

Tacking up is important. Your safety depends on the saddle and bridle being fitted and adjusted correctly.

Tacking up with saddle and bridle

1 Hang your bridle over your left shoulder (if you are right handed) with your arm through the front of it. Put your saddle (with the stirrups run up their leathers and the girth over the seat) over your left forearm with the pommel nearest your elbow. This leaves your right hand free to open doors or gates and maybe deal with the pony.

2 When you reach the pony, put the saddle over the stable door, or a fence rail or gate if he is out. Put the bridle reins over your pony's head so you have control.

3 Stand on his left side at his shoulder with your back to his tail and put your right hand under his throat, taking hold of the bridle cheekpieces with your right hand which then rests on the front of his face just below his eyes. This will bring the bit up level with his teeth. He should open his mouth if you hold the bit across your left hand and press it gently where the teeth meet. If he doesn't, slip your left thumb into the corner of his mouth (where there are no teeth – he can't bite you) and wiggle it about tickling his tongue. He should then open up his mouth and you can gently slip the bit into his mouth.

4 Now hold up the headpiece with your left hand and bring up your right hand to carefully place it over his ears. Make sure his mane is flat and comfortable beneath it, adjust the browband comfortably and fasten first the throatlatch and then the noseband. Now bring the reins back over his head and slip them over your left arm so you have control whilst you saddle up.

2

3

5 Hold the saddle with the pommel in your left hand and the cantle in your right, stand on the pony's near side and place the saddle on top of the withers, sliding it back until the front is behind the withers and shoulder blades: the saddle will probably find its own place on the back.

6 Go round to the off side and bring the girth off the saddle seat so it hangs straight down. Go back to the near side and reach under the pony's belly for the girth, rest the saddle flap on your arm (see below) and fasten the girth to the loosest hole. It is important to girth up (tighten the girth) gradually because ponies can soon become bad tempered if they are made uncomfortable or hurt due to someone girthing up quickly – you wouldn't like it either! Check under the saddle that the straps are straight and the flaps are smooth and not turned under. Pull the flap protectors down over the buckles on the off side.

7 With the reins still over his head, lead your pony to where you are going to mount – ideally from a mounting block or something similar – and girth up one last time before mounting so that you can just slide the flat of your fingers between the girth and the pony's side.

8 Stand in front of the pony facing his tail and, holding each foreleg by the knee, say 'up' and pull them forwards to stretch and smooth out the skin under the girth to make it more comfortable for him and to help prevent girth galls (injuries caused by the skin being pinched). The girth should come a hand's width behind the elbow for comfort.

9 Pull the stirrups down the leathers and mount as you were taught. Girth up another hole and pull the left flap protector over the buckles.

TIP: *Check your girth again after you have been riding for a few minutes; you'll usually have to pull it up a couple of holes. Many ponies will blow themselves out when you try to do up the girth.*

4 Never girth up all at once. Make the process very gradual so that you don't distress or anger your pony, which could make him unco-operative about girthing up in future.

4

Untacking the saddle and bridle

1 Dismount as you have been taught and, with your arm through your reins, undo the girth and run the stirrups up their leathers.

2 Lift (don't drag) the saddle up off the pony's back with both hands, one on the pommel and one on the cantle, catching the girth as it comes across the back and draping it the sweaty side downwards, over the saddle seat. This prevents any grit on the muddy side scratching the seat. Put the saddle on the top of the stable door or stand it against a wall on its pommel with the girth between cantle and wall to prevent the cantle being scratched.

3 Gently but firmly rub the pony's back, both sides, where the saddle and girth have been (called the 'saddle patch' and girth area) to restore the blood circulation. Do not slap the back as this can damage fine blood vessels. Check for rubbed hair or pressure bumps which suggest that your tack does not fit.

4 Undo the noseband and throatlatch in that order then, standing in front of the pony, hold the reins and headpiece together with both hands and

Right: Carry your tack with the bridle hanging off your shoulder and the pommel of the saddle into the crook of your elbow of the same arm, so leaving your other hand free.

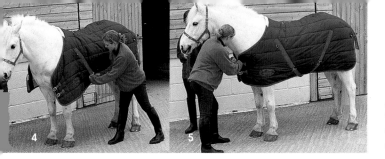

carefully bring them towards you over his ears, allowing him to drop the bit: *never* snatch the bit out of his mouth as this can make him headshy (nervous of having his head handled) and difficult to handle in future.

5 Rub his head where there are any sweaty patches to make him feel better and praise him.

How to rug up

Rugging up properly will ensure that your pony feels comfortable and that the rug cannot slip and cause him to trip.

Rugging up

1 Check that there are no bits of bedding on the inside of the rug which will irritate the pony when it is on; then take the rug with one hand at each end of the seam which runs along the back and place it, bunched together, over the withers.

2 Holding the back edge, pull the rug back in the direction of the hair, so that it comes just in front of the root of the tail and the seam runs directly along the pony's spine.

3 Fasten the surcingles or leg straps *first*, so that if the pony moves and the rug slips it will fall backwards and slide off over his hindquarters where he can step out of it. If you fasten the front first, it will be firmly fastened round his neck only and will slide round, remaining fixed and trailing on the floor where the pony could tread on it and fall down.

4 Sort out the front comfortably and fasten the front breast straps. Do not pull the rug further back as it will slide back a little on its own. The big problem with rugs is keeping them forwards (although well-fitting rugs stay in place reasonably well) so pulling them back will just encourage them to tighten up around the shoulders.

How to remove the rug

1 Undo the front breast straps first for safety.

2 Undo the surcingles or leg straps.

3 Hold the front of the back seam with one hand and the back of it with the other and pull the rug off backwards with both hands over the tail in the direction of the hair. This will leave it folded along the back seam. Fold it once more across the middle so it is more or less in a square and put it somewhere dry where it will not pick up bedding, over the manger or over the door if this is sheltered from the rain.

1 An alternative way of rugging up: lay the folded rug well forward over your pony's loins (the area immediately behind the saddle).

2 Bring the front half forward to well in front of the pony's withers and move it back only slightly so that it remains round the bottom of his neck, not back on his withers.

3 Fasten the surcingles first, not the breast strap, then if something startles the pony and the rug slips, the pony can step out of it easily.

4 You should be able to fit the width of your hand between the surcingles and the pony.

5 Fasten the breast straps last. You should be able to slide your hand easily all round the neckline. Do not be tempted to pull the rug back now: it will slide back of its own accord all too soon and may need frequent refitting to prevent tightening around the neckline.

Taking care of everything

Tack is expensive, and keeping it clean will ensure that it always looks good and will help it to last longer. Get into the habit of cleaning and checking your tack regularly.

Cleaning leather

Wash leather with a clean sponge dipped in a bucket of lukewarm water to which you may add a drop or two of washing up liquid to help remove grease. Squeeze out the excess water and rub firmly all over. Remove stirrup leathers from saddles and hang them on a hook by the buckle so that you can clean them by wrapping your sponge around them and running it up and down.

Hang your bridle on a special hook and clean it whilst it is still buckled up, but with all buckles a couple of holes lower than normal so that you can get at the part of the leather which usually goes behind the buckles and which receives a lot of wear. It's just as quick to take the bridle to pieces and clean it properly, rather than fiddling about.

TIP: *Never mix up your washing and soaping sponges when cleaning your tack, or the whole job will turn into a nightmare.*

Glycerine saddle soap is still the best thing for protecting leather although there are now other creams and lotions. It comes in tins and bars and you rub it with a barely damp sponge (if it is too wet it will lather and not do its job properly), then rub the soap well into the leather with the sponge.

Rub in small circles all over your saddle, up and down straps as when washing, and get plenty of soap on parts behind buckles and where the cheekpieces and reins of your bridle go round the bit rings. The grain, or non-smooth, side of the leather should have plenty of soap and when you have finished use a matchstick or something similar to poke out soap which has clogged in buckle holes in the leather.

Wash your stirrups and bit with a washing sponge in warm, soapy water and rinse very well, particularly the bit. Dry with a rubber, then put everything back together again. Thoroughly wash off any saddle soap which gets on to the mouthpiece.

Occasionally you will need to clean buckles and even stainless steel stirrups with metal polish according to the directions on the tin. Try not to get metal polish on the leather but, if you do, wash it off thoroughly and soap the leather. You can, if you must, clean the cheeks or rings of your bit with metal polish – but never the mouthpiece.

TIP: *It's a good idea as you clean everything to check that there are no cracks in the leather and that the stitching is sound. Catching sight of a weak spot early on and getting it mended can prevent an accident in the future.*

Cleaning synthetics

Follow the care instructions carefully for synthetic items.

Synthetic saddles and bridles are usually cleaned by just washing or wiping down with water and drying off with a towel. Matt synthetics such as saddle seats and panels may just be brushed. You will need to wash synthetic girths properly in warm soapy water and rinse them really well, hanging them up by the buckles to dry.

Most people send rugs to equestrian laundries these days. Quilted synthetic rugs are too bulky to fit into a domestic washing machine and launderettes often will not take them. If you *are* able to wash them yourself, check the instructions carefully. Generally you can wash them in water which is no more than hand hot (maximum 40°C/104°F). Put a little fabric softener in the last rinse and *do not* tumble dry them.

Woollen rugs can be washed in *cold* water on the wool cycle in your washing machine but usually have to be dry cleaned. Oil any leather straps thoroughly first to help protect them, and again when they are dry or returned from the cleaners.

Numnahs and saddle cloths can usually be washed on a lowish temperature in your washing machine: put bandages in an old pillowcase, loosely stitched across the top, to prevent them getting into a hopeless, tight tangle. Synthetic boots can just be swished in warm soapy water in a bucket or the sink, rinsed thoroughly and put to dry.

Above: *Correct procedure for a novice rider and more experienced helper on a public highway. They are to the left with the helper on the pony's right between him and the traffic and both wear reflective clothing.*

handling your pony

It is so easy, when handling a well-behaved pony, working around him, riding him and playing with him, not to realize that he can easily kill you – totally unintentionally, of course, but just because he is much bigger than you and can be frightened easily.

Keeping control

No matter how perfectly behaved your pony is, it is important to always remember that ponies are very strong indeed, very heavy, very fast and easily startled.

Always remember that

◆ a calm mind transmits to the pony and he will pick up on this from you;

◆ if you are firm and persistent with him without getting rough or hyped up he will usually accept that you mean it and will co-operate;

◆ you should have a positive attitude – 'we *are* going through this puddle/gateway/muddy patch sooner or later if I have to sit here all day' – and this, too, transmits to him. Believe in yourself and he will believe in you, too.

General safety

As well as avoiding behaving in a way that might startle your pony, there are a few other things you can do to avoid problems.

◆ Always wear strong boots around ponies to protect your feet. A pony treading on your foot through trainers, wellies or ordinary shoes can break your toes. Do not buy boots with metal toecaps, though, as if the pony treads on these the metal will be pushed down on to your toes and stay there pressing into your foot, making the pain and injury much worse. Buy boots with reinforced leather toecaps: these are quite strong enough and can spring back. Some protective synthetic boots are good, too.

◆ Strictly speaking, you should also wear your hard hat but this is quite impractical for most of us working around the yard. Wear your hat when leading out, though.

◆ Wear gloves when leading a pony, to protect your hands from rope burns, and to give you a better grip.

◆ Do not get crammed into small spaces with your pony. Don't squeeze past him but ask him to move over. Never crawl under his belly ; always walk round him. If he becomes startled in a small space he could squash or trample you, injuring you very seriously.

◆ Be quiet but let your pony know where you are by speaking and running your hands over him.

Above: *Many people advise that a pony be tied up using string on his tie ring, so that if he pulls back in alarm for any reason , the string will break easily and the pony can get free without injuring himself.*

Using your voice

Most people do not use their voices enough: a pony should be just as obedient to voice commands as a well-trained dog. Driving ponies work mainly from the voice and yours can, too. A pony who is obedient to the voice is much safer than one who isn't. Imagine that the pony is getting upset and jigging around and is not listening to your aids to calm down: all you have to say is 'stand' and a well-trained pony will immediately stand still.

All ponies learn commands as youngsters when they are on the lunge: they all know exactly what 'walk on', 'trot', 'canter' and 'whoa' mean and most also understand 'stand' and 'easy' or 'steady'. They also know what 'good boy/girl' means and should also recognize a growling sound or the word 'no' to tell them they are doing something wrong or not wanted.

TIP: *Try to find out from his previous owner what words your pony understands and keep up the good work by using these words regularly.*

Your pony should respond to his name immediately by paying attention or coming to you. Always use it when you approach him and practise getting him to come when called on a long rope or lunge rein, then when loose. Always make a fuss of him when he comes so that he has a good reason to co-operate. When riding, if you want to recall his attention, say his name before giving some other aid.

If you are having problems in getting your pony to understand what you want, ask your instructor for a lesson in voice training and groundwork instead of riding. You'll find it fascinating and a big help in improving obedience and safety.

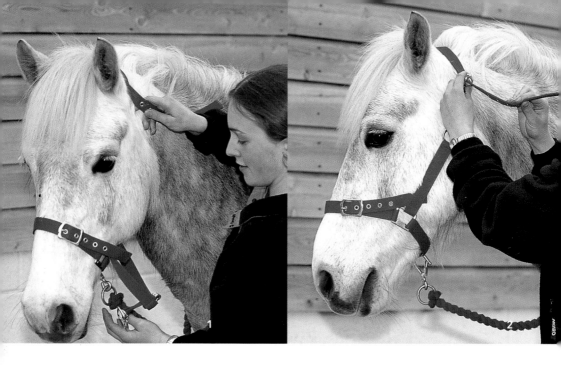

Approaching a pony

Never march straight up to a pony, especially from directly behind him where he cannot see you and might kick out in alarm. Never shout and never thump him in so-called greeting. Ponies do not do this to each other and they hate it from us.

Walk towards his shoulder in a confident, friendly way *speaking his name*. Stand at arm's length and let him sniff the back of your hand, then if he is amenable stroke his shoulder.

Don't give titbits to ponies as they can become peevish when you run out or a real nuisance all the time if they smell something in your pocket. The best reward is to praise him with your voice and stroke him on the face, neck or shoulder.

Stroking is better than patting. Ponies stroke each other with teeth and lips but any sudden, sharp movement like a pat is seen by them to be like a kick which is a sign of displeasure and rejection. If you watch a pony closely, you will see that he prefers being stroked to patted.

If a pony is stabled or tied up, again speak and stand a little way from him, only approaching if he is friendly with ears forward and a soft, welcoming look in his eyes. Otherwise, check with an adult or experienced person who knows him first.

If the pony is loose, speak his name, approach his shoulder and, if he does not turn to face you, stand where you are and try to get him to turn and come to you by speaking and calling him. If this does not work, get expert help.

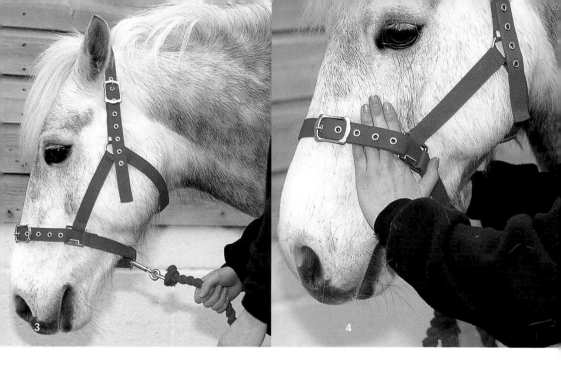

Ponies turned out together in a field can become silly when a human comes on the scene, imagining that there is food somewhere. Get an expert to go with you and separate out your pony.

Working with ponies on the ground

'Perfect ponies' should not give you any trouble but you should still observe pony rules and safety precautions, as discussed above. Stay calm, firm and positive, use your voice, do not get into cramped spaces, wear safe clothing and think ahead about what you are doing and where you are going.

Do not leave objects on the floor near his feet as he could tread on them, break them or hurt himself.

If you have nowhere to tie up a pony, hold his leadrope in one hand and your tools in the other and practise holding the rope and working around him at the same time. It's quite possible.

Putting on a headcollar (halter)

1 Have the headcollar (halter) undone (it fastens on the left side) and hold the left cheekpiece in your left hand and the headpiece in your right hand.
2 Stand by his head with your back to his tail and hold the headcollar under his muzzle, then, carefully but quickly bring it up round his head.
3 Flip the headpiece over his neck behind the ears and fasten it.
4 Clip your leadrope (with the fastening facing away from his head) to the bottom ring of the headcollar under his jaw – and that's that.

1 To put on a headcollar, stand with your back to the tail and, holding the right cheekpiece in your right hand and the left one in your left, bring the noseband carefully round the head. Flick the headpiece over the poll.

2 Next, buckle the headpiece.

3 The fit should be so that the noseband comes at least two fingers' width below the sharp facial bones.

4 You should be able to slide at least the flat of your hand easily all around the head under the straps. It is even better if you are able to fit the width of four fingers between the noseband and throatlatch and the pony's head.

Leading your pony

Ponies should be quite used to being led from both left and right sides, although many are only taught to lead from the left and become quite difficult and puzzled if you lead from the right. Get an expert to help you make your pony 'ambidextrous' – able to be led from both sides. When leading on the road always place yourself between him and the traffic.

TIP: *If you must lead a pony on the road, always use a bridle and have an experienced person with you*.

To lead your pony whichever side you are on, stand just behind his head and a little to the side out of the path of his feet, with your back to his tail – not level with his shoulder as is often taught because if he skips sideways he can easily tread on you.

Hold the leadrope about 15cm or 6in down from his head with the hand nearest to him and hold up the loose end of rope with your other hand. Say 'walk on' and he should go with you.

To lead in a bridle put the bridle on and fasten it normally, then bring the reins right over his head and use them as a leadrope, holding them both together as one rein and leading as described above.

Leading through doorways and gates note which side the door or gate opens. Imagine it is on the right: stand on the left side of the pony holding him in your right hand.

With your left hand, open the gate and *keep hold of it* to control it. Most stable doors open outwards into the yard but gates can open either way.

Tell the pony to 'walk on' and lead him quietly and carefully through, still keeping hold of the gate. Well-behaved ponies will not rush through: if yours does rush he needs retraining.

Bring the pony round you in an arc with your right hand back to the gate and fasten the gate with your left hand. If you are leading your pony into a field, now push him away from you with your right hand, lead him a few metres into the field and turn him around once more to so that he is facing the gate.

Do not let him anticipate being turned loose and break away as this is very dangerous.

Talk to him then, standing more or less facing him, undo his head-collar and slip it quietly down his head, saying something like 'go on, then' which is his signal to go, and step back.

He will turn on his heels and so you will be a full pony's length away and out of harm's way if he kicks up his heels in glee and charges off into the field.

When leading a pony into the stable turn him round to face the door as you fasten it over the top, keeping hold of the pony till the door is fastened.

TIP: *The important point is that your pony must not go till you tell him, otherwise you could be knocked to the ground and trampled.*

Travelling

Loading and unloading ponies is quite safe if you do it properly, although many non-perfect ponies are very difficult about it.

Loading

Remain *calm, firm* and *positive*. Remember, *knowing* that your pony will go straight up that ramp, means he almost certainly *will*. Walk him straight towards the ramp and straight up without hesitating. Tie him to his ring in the trailer at the same length you would on the ground – long enough for comfort but short enough to prevent him getting a leg over the rope. It is usual for the pony to have a haynet to nibble on the journey to keep him occupied.

Unloading

Preferably, your vehicle will have a front-unload side ramp. Untie the pony then have someone take down the breast bar and lead the pony calmly and straight down the ramp. Many ponies go a little quickly so go with him but never let him rush out or leap. If this happens, get an expert to help you with retraining.

Far left: Lead your pony out of his stable straight, not at an angle, in case he bangs his hips (or you!) against the door jamb.

Top left: Learning to lead a pony through a gateway, with an expert helper on hand. Control the gate with one hand and the pony with the other.

Middle left: Turn the pony around and back to face the gate which you are still holding to prevent it swinging on to you both.

Bottom left: Fasten the gate properly before turning the pony loose.

Below: Dressing a pony for travelling. Here, his travelling boots are being fitted.

Bottom: Lead your pony directly towards the ramp, really believing that he will go in, and he probably will.

If the pony has to back down the ramp, which he may be unsure about, untie him first then get someone to undo the breeching strap or bar behind him. Stand facing his head slightly to one side and say 'back', giving him a gentle push on the breast. He must be allowed to take his time, to turn his head a little so he can see where he is going and to feel his way with his hind feet. Someone should be outside to guide him down. Keep *calm, firm* and *positive* and don't rush. If you have problems, get expert help.

Tying up your pony

You should always tie your pony to a string loop through the metal ring so that if he panics the string loop will break and he can get free. Never use binder twine as it is too strong to break easily.

Pass your rope through the string loop and tie it with a half bow in what is called a 'quick-release' safety knot. Get an expert to show you just how to do this. The knot is left with a free end of rope which you just pull down firmly to undo the pony immediately.

Various safety catches are available from most saddlers which allow for quick release in an emergency.

There will be a loop of rope on the knot, and some people pass the free end of rope through this to stop the pony learning how to untie the knot. However, if you do this and then need to undo the pony quickly you have to fiddle getting the end free first, wasting valuable seconds. If you, or the pony, pulls the free end when it is through the loop the knot will tighten up so that you may not be able to undo it at all – a very dangerous situation.

Don't tie up your pony when...

Sometimes it is far safer for someone to hold the pony for treatment of some kind rather than have him tied up. It's not a good idea to tie up your pony when:

◆ The pony is one who tends to pull back hard on his rope causing damage and injury to himself, buildings and bystanders. Ponies like this need holding, or expert retraining.
◆ In a situation in which the pony may become alarmed or fractious, such as shoeing, veterinary treatment, clipping and so on. Get someone knowledgeable to hold the pony in these situations. Ponies should behave well at these times but many do not.
◆ Never tie up a pony and leave him for some time, such as on a showground or while you go indoors for a coffee.
◆ Never tie up a pony when there are other, loose ponies around, such as in a field. They might bully him or he might panic.

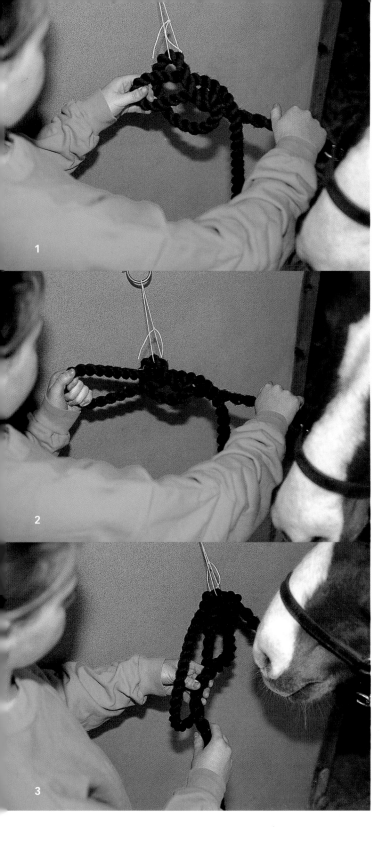

1 *Tying a quick-release knot can be tricky so get someone to show you how. Here, the rope has been passed through the string tie-ring and looped into a half bow.*

2 *Tighten the half bow, leaving the loose end hanging down.*

3 *Do not thread the loose end through the loop, as is being done here. If you or the pony pull on it, it will tighten the knot and it will no longer be quick-release, which is the whole point of this knot.*

How to pick up feet

Forefeet stand at the shoulder facing the tail and, if on the right, run your right hand from his shoulder all the way down the back of his front leg. Get hold of the fetlock, give a firm but not rough upward pull and say 'up'. When he lifts the foot, hold the toe with your left hand and slide your right hand under the front of the hoof and coronet to support it while you pick it out with your left hand.

1 *To pick up a left forefoot, stand facing the tail and run your left hand down the back of the leg.*

2 *Pull on the back of the fetlock, saying 'up' at the same time. Hold the hoof with your right hand while your left lets go of the fetlock and slides around to replace the right.*

3 *Support the hoof with your left hand and work with your right.*

Hind feet stand facing the tail at the hip and, if on the left side, run your left hand from his hip down the outside of his upper leg, then around the inner side of his hock and inner side of his cannon to the fetlock so that his leg is in front of your arm. Then if he kicks (which he will usually do backwards) he cannot pull you with him and you can just let go.

Grasp the fetlock firmly but not roughly, give an upward pull and say 'up'. Hold the toe with your right hand while you slide your left under the front of the hoof and coronet to hold the foot. Work with your right hand.

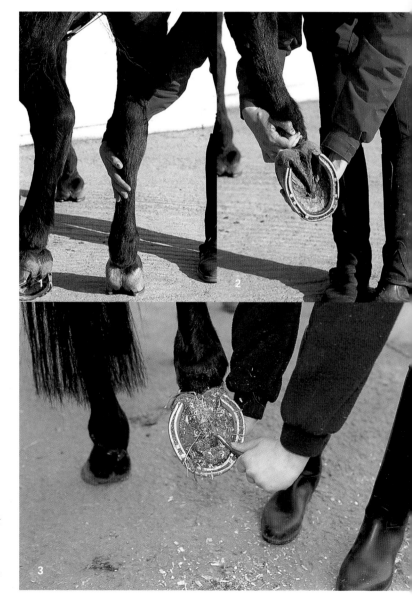

1 *To pick up a right hind foot, stand facing the tail and run your right hand down the inside of the leg.*

2 *Pull on the back of the fetlock, while simultaneously saying 'up'. Hold the hoof with your left hand while your right hand releases the fetlock and slides round to replace the left hand.*

3 *Work with your left hand, while supporting the hoof with your right.*

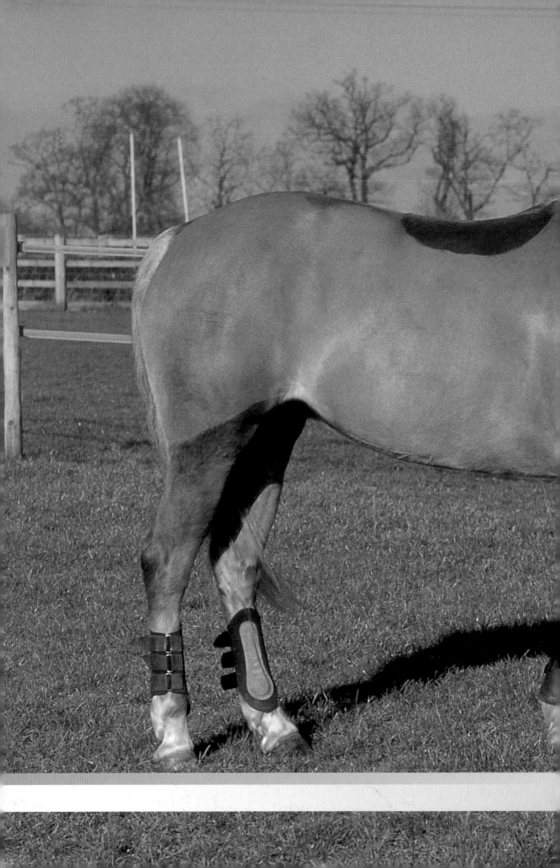

clipping and trimming

Many ponies are never clipped or trimmed and are fine. Sometimes, owners go overboard with clipping and trimming, to the pony's detriment.

Clipping is done in winter to remove the winter coat by using electric clippers so that the pony does not sweat too much during work, feel very uncomfortable, perhaps become chilled later and maybe lose weight because of it.

Trimming tidies up (usually shortening and thinning) the mane and forelock, maybe fining down the top of the tail and perhaps shortening it from the bottom.

Which ponies should be clipped?

Whether or not you clip and trim depends on how you keep your pony and what you do with him. If he is a native-type pony or cob and lives out in winter, he almost certainly should not be clipped unless you can give him a good turnout rug and bring him into shelter at night. If he is not working at all hard there is no point in clipping him but a tidy up may smarten his appearance. If he *is* working hard and may sweat a lot, you could have him clipped.

If he is a finer-bred pony not working hard, he should not be clipped – even with a turnout rug he needs all the coat he can get. If he *is* working hard, a suitable clip will make him more comfortable.

Clipping

Clipping is a skilled job and many ponies dislike the process although many are well-behaved. If you only have one or two ponies, it is not worth buying a clipping machine. Pay an expert to come and do it for you: they advertise in local papers and magazines from autumn onwards.

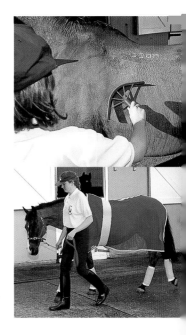

TIP: *If you do want to clip, wait till the pony's winter coat has 'set' (fully grown – during November) and you can probably get away with one clip for the whole winter.*

What sort of clip?

Almost all ponies, including hard-working ones, do very well with what is called a trace clip. The hair is removed from the underside of the pony – under the neck, breast, belly and round the tops of the legs – up to the height of the traces on a harness pony. The leg hair is left on.

There are 'high' and 'low' trace clips in which the line is taken higher to remove more hair or lower to leave more hair, according to the pony's type and how hard he is working.

The person who comes to clip your pony will judge his type and discuss his work with you, so you can decide on what is best. Just remember that the more hair you remove the colder the pony will feel, the more food, rugs and shelter he will need and probably the livelier he will become.

Preparation

Make sure your pony is clean and dry before clipping him otherwise dirt will blunt and clog the clipper blades and they will pull painfully. Damp hair also tends to pull on the blades. Anything which hurts will make the pony difficult to clip in future. Some ponies even need sedating before clipping – but not perfect ones!

Give the pony a good grooming or shampoo the day before and have his rugs (blankets) clean and ready.

When the 'clipper' arrives, he or she will probably prefer you to hold the pony rather than tie him up. In any case, have a haynet full and ready for him to nibble to keep him occupied and take his mind off the process. However good your pony is, few of them seem to find being clipped enjoyable.

Clipping usually takes place in a stable or special grooming box. The floor should be dry and non-slip. Clippers are electric and do not mix well with damp! You need a safe electricity point and must watch to see that the pony does not tread on the flex. You can pile excess flex into a dry bucket.

As clipping proceeds, put the rug over the pony's loins and hindquarters to stop him fidgeting if he feels chilly. A trace clip takes about half an hour to do.

After clipping, give the clipped areas a good brushing with the body brush to remove broken bits of hair and help stop the pony feeling itchy. Remove hair from the floor and put it in the dustbin.

Remember to make sure your pony has as much fibrous feed as he wants as this will help him keep warm and get over the sudden shock of losing some of his inbuilt central heating.

Above: *This little pony has been given a 'bib' clip which is very useful for woolly ponies not in regular hard work.*

Left: *Clipped animals need to be dried off quickly. Here, a sweat scraper is being used to get excess water out of the coat rapidly.*

Left: *This is a mesh cooler rug or anti-sweat sheet. The mesh creates tiny air flows against the skin and, in hot weather, helps cool off an animal quicker. Clipped animals, though, which work in cold weather, shouldn't wear these rugs, as they can cool off ponies too quickly and they may become chilled.*

ears and whiskers

Never clip the hair out of the insides of the pony's ears as this is needed to help catch dirt and bits to stop them falling into the ear.

Most people believe that the long whiskers around eyes and muzzle should definitely not be removed. These are like antennae which the pony uses to feel around, particularly in the dark, and are an important part of his sensory equipment. Some people think their removal improves a pony's appearance; but you would never do it to your dog, rabbit or cat, so why your pony?

Trimming

Trimming can be quite uncomfortable for a pony but there are now special combs and other gadgets which make it relatively painless. The person who clips your pony can probably be called on all year round to give your pony an occasional trim. You can also pay for a lesson in how to do this yourself and page 139 has photographs of how to do it.

Shortening hair

The important points to remember are that, if you are showing in breed classes, you are not supposed to trim your cob or pony at all although a little careful trimming will not be noticed! Over-long manes and tails not only look silly but get very messy and you can simply shorten them by snapping off the ends of the hair between your finger and thumb which gives a natural look.

Banging a tail

For ponies of no special breed, a 'banged' tail looks smart if well done. This menas cutting off the bottom of the tail in one big snip with large, very sharp shears or scissors so it is squared off. Remember that when your pony moves he will hold up his tail so that the bottom edge of the bang will slope down towards his back legs at an angle and look awful.

To avoid this, there are two ways of banging a tail:
- Put your hand right round all the hairs at the end of the dock and run it down the tail to a little longer than you want it (mid-cannon

Right: *Decide each day whether the weather is bad enough to warrant putting a rug on your clipped pony. Most ponies are fine in dry, still weather, but they hate wind and rain.*

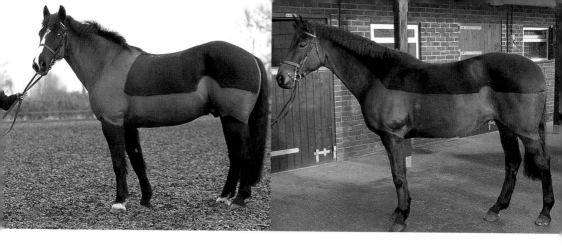

length suits most ponies). Keep a steady downward pull on the hair. Position the shears above your hand, pointing them directly between the pony's hind legs and slightly upwards towards his hocks. Make a single bold snip and let go. When your pony holds his tail naturally, the bang should now be dead level with the ground.

◆ Get a friend to place his or her forearm under the pony's dock at the top to hold it up and in a curve, as it is when he is moving. Run your hand down the hairs again, as described above, but this time make your snip absolutely level with the ground. Then let your friend move her arm away and let go of the tail: when your pony moves his bang should be level with the ground and look very smart.

To trim the ears
Hold the edges of the ears together and just snip off (with sharp scissors with rounded, safe ends) the hair which protrudes beyond the edges. That's all you need to do (see note on page 133).

To trim the fetlocks
If you are sure you really want to do this, take a coarse-toothed comb and, ideally, rounded fetlock scissors, comb the hair up towards the roots and snip off the hairs from between the teeth of the comb. Do not clip the fetlocks as they will look really amateurish. Again, with native show ponies and cobs of particular breeds you are not allowed to remove fetlock hair: instead, make a point of having it very clean and brushed out to make your pony look really good and appealing.

TIP: *Remember that natural hair or 'feather', as it is called, on all ponies and cobs is meant to help protect the lower legs from wet in winter. However, if the pony does get mud fever, the hair will have to be cut off to treat it.*

Above left: *This is a blanket clip. A patch is left on the back roughly where an under-blanket would go, although this clip is rather far back at the front. The blanket clip is suitable for hard-working ponies as quite a lot of hair has been clipped off.*

Above: *This type of clip is correctly termed a 'chaser' (steeplechaser) clip. It is similar to a trace clip, which reaches up to where the traces would go on a driving pony, except that the head hair has also been removed. A chaser clip is all most ponies will need unless they are working very hard.*

shows and
competitions

These can either be great fun, or fraught with stress and worry. Not everyone has a competitive streak, and if you find they freak you out maybe they are not your scene; you could be doing something more rewarding and relaxing with your pony such as hacking, and lessons to improve your technique and safety. If, though, competition provides you with a 'buzz' and a challenge, go out and enjoy yourself, but remember to put your pony's welfare before any prizes he may win for you.

Disciplines and turnout

Earlier in this book we looked at the different sports and activities in which you can take part with your pony – in-hand (at halter), ridden or driven, competitive and non-competitive. All activities have certain requirements for turnout (what you and your pony wear) and this contributes not only to appearance but also to safety. In some disciplines, if you are not dressed correctly you won't win anything no matter how well your pony goes, and you may even not be allowed to compete.

.   The subject of correct turnout is very complicated and whole books have been written about it. The best way to learn is to study the turnout of the winners and highest-placed participants in your chosen sport. Most ruling bodies can also supply full details on what clothing and tack may and may not be worn and they differ between classes so make sure you do your homework on this point. Rules are quite relaxed at smaller shows except where safety is concerned but at larger ones things are more strict. In potentially dangerous sports, say where jumping is involved, you must wear correct, safe gear or you will not be allowed to compete.

TIP: *Check your pony's shoes at least a week or two before the show and get the farrier to visit if they need attention. It's no good finding out that he has a loose shoe the day before the competition.*

show tips

Don't be afraid to ask someone in authority what you should be wearing and how it should fit.

When showing, it is more correct to dress down rather than up. It looks sillier, for example, to wear a black or navy showing coat when everyone else is in tweed than to wear a tweed one when everyone else is dressed up smartly. Similarly, your pony wearing a coloured browband when everyone else has a plain one will look more out of place than to have him in a plain one when everyone else has a coloured one.

Remember that it is the pony who is being judged and should be the centre of attention, not you, so you must be dressed smartly and correctly but *discreetly*. Flashiness is always in bad taste.

Left: *Check beforehand that your competition or show venue has water laid on, as ponies working hard at a competition will need frequent drinks. If water is not supplied, take a large container full of water with you.*

Below: *To shorten and thin the mane, use a mane comb to backcomb the hair up to the roots.*

Bottom: *Press your thumb or finger (whichever you find easiest) against the top of the comb and pull out only a very few hairs at a time. Modern mane-trimming gadgets take the pain out of pulling manes.*

The day before

To save rushing around on the morning of the show, there are a number of tasks that should be done a day or more beforehand.

◆ If going to a show, you may wish to shampoo your pony. Remember that if you wash his mane and tail too close to a show day they may be too clean and slippery to plait up well (if you are plaiting up) so do them a few days before and don't do them again when shampooing the rest of him.

◆ If you are entering some other competition, a really thorough grooming will make your pony look good, perhaps just washing white socks.

◆ Clean all tack and other equipment if not done before.

Make sure you have a list of everything you are taking with you and have it repaired, clean and ready to load into your trailer or horsebox the next morning. In general, you will need:

◆ Transport vehicle in good order and filled up with fuel: oil, water and tyres checked.

◆ Directions to venue and map.

◆ Paperwork - all insurances, breakdown cards or documents, entry forms, vaccination certificates, registration papers and so on.

◆ First-aid kit for you and your pony.

◆ Saddle/s and bridle/s, in-hand (at halter) headgear and leadreins/ropes, boots.

◆ Rug/s (blankets) or sheet/s.

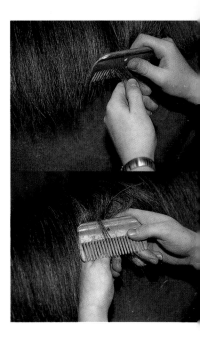

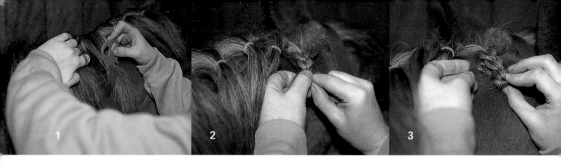

- ◆ Grooming and plaiting/braiding kits.
- ◆ Haynets, dry feed and water in large containers (because some ponies will not drink strange water away from home; also not all smaller venues have water supplies), buckets.
- ◆ Pony's travelling gear – poll guard, headcollar (halter) and rope, rug/blanket, boots, tail bandage and guard.
- ◆ Your own clothes – hats, coats, jodphurs or breeches, shirt, ties, gloves, socks, maybe spare underwear in case you get soaked, other clothes of your choice if showing in-hand (at halter), wellies if wet, plastic bags for keeping things clean.

Try to treat the pony fairly normally, although he's bound to sense something is in the air. Turn him out in the morning and prepare him in the afternoon. Feed him as normal. If he usually lives out but is spending the night indoors to keep him clean, make sure all possible ventilation points are open or he could sweat up and be miserable.

Below left: A mane comb can be used to pull out the hair at the sides of your pony's dock but most people simply use their fingers and pull out a few hairs a day to prevent soreness.

Below: This spotted pony is sporting a neatly pulled tail.

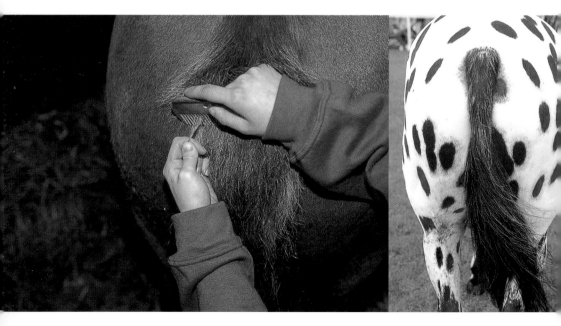

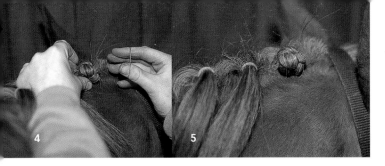

1 *Plaiting manes is time consuming so allow yourself plenty of time. First damp the hair and separate it into equal locks according to how many plaits you want.*

2 *Plait evenly and not too tightly down to the bottom.*

3 *Turn under the very bottom of the plait and either wrap thread or a very small elastic band around it. Then fold the bottom of the plait up and under to the crest of the neck as many times as needed to make a 'button'.*

4 *Using needle and thread, sew the button in place. Elastic bands (matching your pony's mane colour) will do if small and tight, but these are not as secure.*

5 *This is what a finished button plait looks like. There are different types for different equestrian sports.*

Below: *Prepare the trailer with bedding and hay before loading up your pony for a journey.*

On the day

Being organized will help you and your pony to stay as calm as possible.
- Plait up/braid the pony, if appropriate.
- Load everything into the vehicle. The pony should be dressed and loaded last.
- Aim to leave in *plenty* of time. If you rush you will be all wound up on arrival. Remember that travelling is always stressful for the pony. For every hour travelled, he needs an hour of recovery before he is really ready to work, but few ponies get this.
- The driver should aim to keep the vehicle at as constant a speed and on as straight a line of travel as possible to minimize the pony having to constantly use, and tire, his muscles to keep his balance. Make sure the driver accelerates, brakes and corners *very* gradually and avoids bumps and pot holes.

TIP: *If you are hacking to the show, leave plenty of time for your journey. It's not a good idea to arrive in a nervous state with your pony in a lather because you have had to hurry.*

On arrival

Once you arrive, it is important to get your pony settled comfortably and get through the formalities.
- Have ready any papers needed to admit you to the showground, to show at the gate.
- Someone should go immediately to the secretary's tent to report your presence, enter if not done already, collect your number and so on.
- Unload the pony, take off travelling gear and offer him a drink.
- If raining put on waterproof sheet/neck cover.
- Take the pony to some grass and see if he wants to stale. Let him have some grass now and throughout the day as he will be used to it and needs to keep some passing through his system.
- Walk him calmly round to stretch his legs and relax his muscles..
- If the weather is very wet, remove some partitions in the vehicle and reload him, if there is nowhere under cover to stand, and let him have his haynet.
- Remove the haynet an hour before hard work, tack up and work him in.

- Between classes, keep the pony warm and dry inside the vehicle if the weather is bad or, depending on the venue and competition, in a stable you have booked ahead. If it is hot, find somewhere outdoors and in the shade to stand with him to keep him calm, *cool* and relaxed.
- Do let him have a little feed and/or haynet or grass, and certainly water, between every class to keep him comfortable, settled and to keep his energy up.

TIP: *Never tie him up somewhere with a haynet and leave him. Someone should be near him and your vehicle all the times, for security and safety reasons.*

After work
- Take out any plaits/braids as soon as possible for the pony's comfort.
- Offer him feed/grass/water before the journey and make sure there is a haynet in the vehicle for his homeward journey.
- Sweep out any droppings from the vehicle.
- Load up all your gear – including all the rosettes and trophies he has won for you!
- Dress the pony for travelling and load him.

Once you are home
- Walk the pony round a little if he is going to be stabled, to loosen him up.
- Check him carefully all over for any injuries and treat them accordingly.
- Give him water, normal feed and hay.
- Don't pester him by unnecessary grooming: if he is very muddy wash him off and put on 'drying' clothes such as stable bandages and breathable rug, and check him later.
- If he is going back to his field, turn him out as soon as you have checked and fed him, provided he is well. Rug up or not, as usual.

The next day
- Check your pony as early as possible for tiredness, injuries, wounds, failure to eat up his supper, or to drink water and so on. If there is anything at all you are not happy about, get expert help and do not hesitate to ring the vet (veterinarian) if you are worried.
- If the pony has worked hard, let him rest next day, but walk him in-hand (at halter) and trot him up to check for lameness or undue stiffness. A relaxing day in the field with his friends is probably what he would like most.

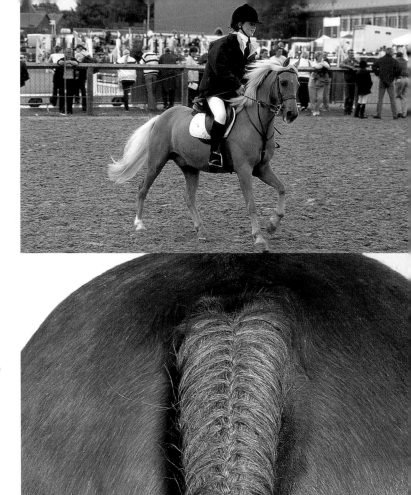

Top right: *Ponies can look lovely and natural without plaits, as long they are discreetly trimmed and very clean. Plaits are not normally allowed in breed classes.*

Left:
1 *To plait, braid or lace a tail, the tail must be completely unpulled and a natural length. Take two locks, one from each side.*

2 *Cross them over and hold them firmly, but not painfully tight!*

3 *Take in another lock from the right and cross it over the left lock which is already in your right hand.*

4 *Keep taking in locks from each side and do a three-strand plait, reaching approximately two-thirds of the way down your pony's dock. At the bottom, continue plaiting the hair you have, without taking in any more hair, so that you have a long plait. Turn under the end and wrap thread around it, then turn up the bottom to the point where you stopped taking in locks of hair.*

Right: *Sew down the centre of your plait-loop so that it looks like one thicker plait. Wrap the thread around the end and sew through it three or four times to finish off. This is the final, very smart, result.*

A novice, whether adult or child, should *never* buy a badly-behaved pony. They do not have the skills to correct him or her. Bad behaviour and lack of discipline in an animal as strong as a pony can be very dangerous and you need to know how to cope with it. This chapter on training is not included with the intention of teaching readers how to train a pony because this is specialized work, but it will give you some idea of what is involved in training.

What is involved in training?

When we talk of 'training' an older pony, we should remember that ponies know perfectly well how to be ponies! They know how to walk, trot, canter, gallop, stop, jump and also rein back (move backwards) and move sideways. Their problems come when we sit on their backs and completely upset their balance, then expect them to be able to do all the usual things while carrying us.

Of course, everyone has to start somewhere and can learn how to train ponies by having lessons from an experienced teacher.

Timescale

It takes years for a pony or horse to become fully trained and many never reach that standard. At the famous Spanish Riding School in Vienna, very expert and capable riders take six years to train the young Lipizanner stallions from first being ridden to being able to perform the difficult and strenuous High School work expected of them.

Of course, we don't expect this of our ponies, but the following gives an idea of what a normal training programme might involve.

Foals

Ideally, every foal should gradually be taught from a few days old to lead in-hand (at halter) alongside its mother (dam), to answer voice requests from humans and to be groomed gently and handled all over, including picking up the legs and feet for cleaning and, from about three months, in preparation for their first visit from the farrier. Within a few months, he should learn to be tied up for a few minutes (but not left alone), turned out and caught again (with his dam). As he approaches weaning (at about eight months) he should learn to spend short periods (from a few minutes to an hour) without mother nearby as they approach weaning age at around eight months.

After weaning, the foal should lead independently from his dam, should be well mannered and obeying voice commands and light touches on his body to position him, move him around and so on. He should stand obediently for grooming and farriery and for the vet.

The trainer starts off lungeing by standing quite close to the pony.

As the pony becomes more proficient, the trainer stands further away.

Long-reining/long-lining is more versatile than lungeing. This is the traditional method, with the trainer standing a good way behind the pony who has long reins passed down his sides through stirrups.

Working ponies in hand is enjoyable and fun. This pony is learning to watch where he puts his feet by walking over poles.

Most ponies love learning to jump. This little grid of cross-poles encourages the pony to lift his legs, be careful where he puts his feet and also gives him fun while he is learning.

Yearlings

Between the ages of one and two, the youngster continues to learn stable manners. He should stand quietly when tied up for several minutes, lead willingly and obediently around the stud/stud farm, be groomed and gradually become accustomed to motorized traffic and travelling.

Two-year-olds

Between two and three years, the youngster should be leading very obediently in hand around the stud and, perhaps, out and about around the local, quiet lanes and tracks or trails, with expert handlers and an older, very well-behaved horse to set an example. He should be introduced to long-reining which gives more control than leading: this consists of two long reins attached to a special halter called a lungeing cavesson (or even to a bridle with mild bit), one rein running along each side of the pony and held by a trainer who walks behind and/or to the side of him. (There are other methods: this is the traditional English-style method.)

The pony should be used to stepping over poles and varied ground, including going through shallow water following a trained horse or pony. He can be mouthed (introduced to having a bit in his mouth) and be accustomed to wearing a saddle, all of which instil extra discipline. However, the old practice of trussing a youngster up into a 'shape' (with his head strapped in to his saddle or a roller) and leaving him standing in stable or paddock should definitely not be undertaken as it is cruel, causes cramp and pain in the muscles and does nothing to encourage a willing attitude or correct physical development.

'Breaking in' or 'starting'

The unfortunate term 'breaking in' is still used traditionally and implies breaking a horse's spirit which is not the idea at all. More modern methods use the word 'starting' and are based more on our adopting the horse's body language to communicate with him. This gets quicker and more effective results.

The traditional way is to put the youngster (three years of age is normal – breaking too young damages the pony and shortens his working life) on a long rein called a lunge rein with the trainer on one end and an assistant leading the pony round on a large circle. If he is obedient to the voice in-hand, lungeing is just one logical step onwards.

He learns to respond to 'walk on', 'trot', 'canter', 'whoa' and 'stand'. Gradually, the assistant takes less and less of a rôle and finally only the trainer works the pony from the middle of a large circle.

When he works obediently and enthusiastically on both reins (in both directions) some trainers will then use a method called long-reining (long-lining) in which the pony has a long rein on both sides of him and the trainer can work more in different shapes, not just circles.

You can achieve quite a high standard of training and muscular development with long-reining.

Backing

Once good discipline has been obtained, the youngster, who will already have been accustomed to a saddle and bridle, will have a lightweight rider introduced. The pony is still held by his familiar trainer; at first the rider will simply pat the saddle, then lean on the pony's back and then over the saddle. Eventually, he or she will put a leg over the saddle but remain leaning down so as not to frighten the pony with his upper body suddenly appearing above and behind the pony (ponies can see behind them).

The next stage is for the pony and rider, still on the lunge, to work through all the gaits – walk, trot and canter – in obedience to commands from the trainer, but the rider gives the pony physical commands (called 'aids') to coincide with the trainer's spoken ones, so that the pony associates the two.

Eventually, the trainer will take a lesser rôle and the rider speaks to the pony instead and uses the physical aids. The end result is when the pony will work well from just the physical aids and off the lunge.

The youngster can start to be gently ridden for very short periods (up to half an hour) about three or four days a week. Long-reining should continue and many people also school (train) youngsters on the lunge rein now – a long rein running from the lungeing cavesson. He can start popping over very low obstacles, perhaps loose rather than lunged or long-reined, and should be used to being properly shod. He can go on outings for experience – in quiet areas with a very well-trained older horse or pony for company.

Other techniques

Some people like to loose-school ponies, that is work them in a 'lane' or other enclosed area just using the voice and body language. Most ponies enjoy this and it can be used for flatwork and jumping.

Schooling over poles on the ground, ridden, in-hand or on lunge or long-reins, is also fun and makes the pony think where he is putting his feet and to watch where he is going. It also encourages him to work with his head down, stretching his neck and back muscles and going in a correct, rounded shape or 'outline'.

Little jumps can be started after a line of poles which most ponies enjoy but young ones should jump only tiny jumps (0.3m/1ft maximum) a couple of times a week. More serious jumping can be started at four years old but remember that over-working a pony when young shortens his working life, wears him out and is both unfair and bad horsemanship.

Continuing training

Training can continue for a lifetime, but a pony is regarded as well-trained when he is reliably obedient to the rider's aids, does not object or play up (unless genuinely frightened), and goes correctly, at which point the owner should continue to take regular lessons with the pony from a

Right, from top:
This jump has a pole placed as a ground line to make the jump easier and more substantial-looking, and so provides encouragement to pony and rider.

Leading your pony between a narrow alley of poles placed at angles aids obedience and makes the pony think carefully about his body position.

All ponies should come when called, but few actually do. Call your pony's name and give gentle pulls on the rein to get him to come to you. Praise him as soon as he takes a step towards you to encourage him. Do not give food treats as a reward: just praise him with your voice and stroke his neck.

Loose jumping in moderation is good for ponies and most love it.

This pair is becoming quite expert at small jumps, in good style.

stumbling

Ponies can often find it difficult to cope with putting their feet in the right places when being ridden and being asked to do certain things at certain times. Young or untrained ('green') ponies often trip, stumble and sometimes even fall because of this.

good teacher. This point is unlikely to be reached in less than a year, and that is with expert training which many ponies do not get.

Many people do not know what to aim for when trying to train a pony so lessons from an expert will teach them how to go on and what they should be doing for that particular pony as regards developing his mind, his body and furthering his experience and abilities.

Many teachers are qualified but some excellent ones are not. They must all have insurance, however, and you must have a teacher/trainer with whom you get on. If any trainer does anything to your pony, or tries to make you do something which you are not happy about, remember that you do not have to do it. Find a good, sympathetic teacher and persevere with lessons and learn as much as you can.

Ponies and riding are a lifelong, fascinating hobby. Nobody ever learns everything about the subject which is why it is a constant challenge and inspiration.

Problem solving

Sometimes, when ponies change hands and go to a new home, they are quick to weigh up their new people and may start doing naughty things which they could not get away with in their old home. Sometimes, they start what appears to be misbehaving because they sense that their new rider is not as good as the previous one and the pony may actually be feeling insecure, not quite as safe as with a more experienced rider. Most ponies need leadership. Bad behaviour, whether caused by naughtiness, insecurity or fear, may include the following:

◆ Napping/jibbing/setting (the pony refuses to go forwards and may actually run backwards)
◆ Rearing (the pony stands up on his hind legs which is one of the most dangerous things a pony can do)
◆ Bucking (the pony leaps up in the air off all four legs, usually with his head down and sometimes twisting around in the air)
◆ Running away or pulling hard and going much too fast when ridden
◆ Biting and kicking
◆ Barging you out of the way
◆ Refusing jumps (usually due to pain, uncertainty or bad riding)
◆ Being frightened of going through water – or just not liking getting his legs wet and so refusing to go through

If your pony starts misbehaving for whatever reason, remember that it can make him dangerous in certain circumstances and you need to get him retrained by an expert. This is certainly no job for a child or an inexperienced adult. Any qualified instructor should be able to undertake this for you and may come to the pony's home to do so, and some professional stables take in animals for retraining. It is important that whoever does this work also trains you to cope with the pony as otherwise, once left to your own devices again, the bad behaviour will probably return.

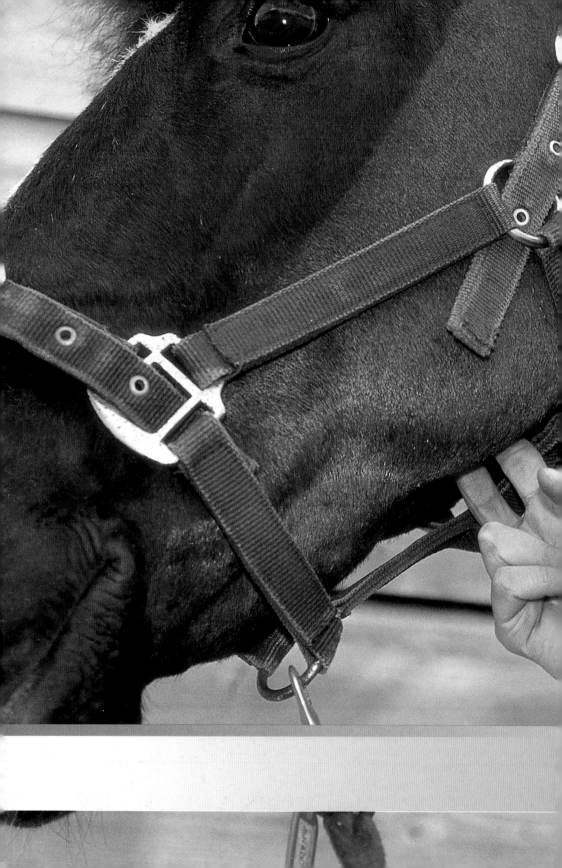

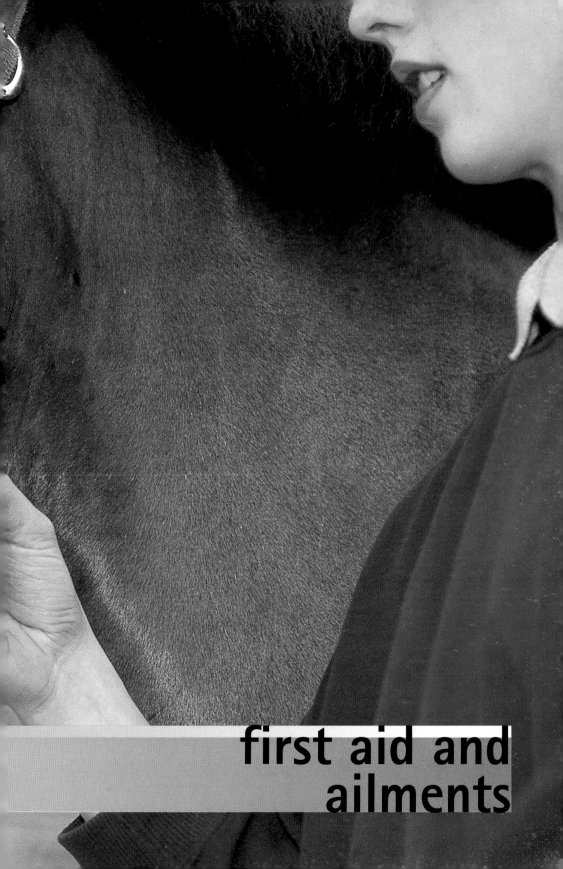

first aid and
ailments

Ponies sometimes become sick or injured – you can't avoid it, however careful you are. Ponies are flesh and blood like the rest of us and can feel illness and pain just as badly. Then they will need the attention of a veterinary surgeon (veterinarian) and may also need nursing at home; in that case, unless you keep your pony at a very good professional yard where you can be sure the staff will nurse him properly, someone in your family may have to take time off work to look after him because he may need frequent attention. Just because he is an animal and not a person, he cannot be neglected or be expected to get better on his own. In rare cases, he may need to go to a veterinary hospital.

Insurance

Veterinary attention of any kind is costly, but some diseases, investigations to find out what is wrong or serious accidents can be very expensive to put right, and ongoing care may be needed for some time. To be sure you can afford to pay for this, you should take out insurance to cover veterinary fees before things go wrong: if you wait until this happens and then try to get insurance, the insurance company will not cover the current problem either now or in the future.

Insurance can be very complicated and there are good and bad companies. Find a reputable company by asking other owners' advice. You may see leaflets in your veterinary surgery advertising a particular company, which should mean that the company is reputable, although vets will not actually recommend companies.

Signs of good health

Get to know what your pony's health is usually like: it will help you to spot problems earlier.

- Your pony should be interested in his surroundings and seem calm but alert, neither very dull nor hyped up. His ears should be pricked forward towards whatever is interesting him, although they may relax more sideways when he is resting or dozing.
- His eyes should be bright, clear and full with no discharges, redness or swelling; he shouldn't rub or close either of his eyes frequently.
- His skin and coat should be bright and 'alive', even in a grass-kept pony, with no swellings, sores, wounds, rashes, excessive scurf or scabs. It should be possible to move it around easily over the ribs with the flat of your hand and the pony should not frequently rub or bite himself to relieve irritation. The coat should not be stiff and

help yourself

As well as a good first-aid kit, you must also have a detailed, *up-to-date* veterinary book for horse owners.

Read it from cover to cover and keep it handy. Ideally, have a copy at your yard and a copy at home so you can always refer to it.

Make yourself as familiar as possible with signs of good health and abnormalities and especially with first-aid techniques and emergency situations.

Above: *A shiny coat, bright eyes and an interest in life are signs of good health.*

Below: *Young foals go downhill quickly when sick: keep a careful eye on all foals and ring your vet if there are any problems.*

Bottom: *Once you've been shown how to do it by an expert, taking your pony's temperature is not difficult.*

harsh, dull or 'staring' (seeming to stand a little away from the skin), although a winter coat will stand up a little as part of keeping warm.

◆ Movement should be fluid and loose, with even strides and no reluctance to move; the pony should be able to reach right down to graze and around his sides with his head and neck, and also to lie down, roll and get up again without difficulty.

◆ Appetite and thirst should be healthy and normal. A pony who refuses food may well be sickening for something (but check that the quality of the food is good) as may one who drinks either a great deal or very little (again check that the water and container are really clean). Automatic drinkers are no use in this respect unless they have meters telling you how much has been drunk. Watch the pony regularly to check that he eats and drinks in a normal way and does not appear to be having difficulties.

◆ Droppings and urine: a pony will do about eight to twelve lots of droppings in twenty-four hours. If on grass they will be green and looser than those of a stabled pony, which are usually khaki in colour and formed into apple-shaped balls which just break on hitting the ground. Urine may be clear or cloudy and is usually a yellow colour. Variations from the above could indicate sickness.

◆ Breathing should be silent and difficult to detect when the pony is at rest. A slight watery discharge from the nostrils is normal but a thick one, especially if it is yellow or greenish, indicates a problem. A discharge of blood is certainly abnormal.

◆ After rolling, the pony should shake: if he does not it may indicate abdominal discomfort which could mean colic.

◆ Sweating is normal after work but if a resting pony sweats it could simply mean that he is too hot or that he is sick or in pain. Cold sweating indicates shock and exhaustion.

Vital signs

These are certain pointers which are reliable guides to your pony's state of health:

Body temperature this is about 38°C or 100.4°F in a resting pony who has not recently been exercised or galloping around his field. Buy a veterinary thermometer from your vet (veterinarian) and always keep it in its case. There are plastic safety ones and digital ones but they are not so accurate as the normal glass ones. Shake the thermometer so that the mercury falls below the scale, lubricate the end by dipping it in Vaseline or spitting on it and, standing close to the hindquarters near the tail on, say, the left side, bring the tail towards you with your left hand and insert the thermometer carefully into the anus with your right hand. The bulb should lie against the wall of the rectum; *do not* move it around or force it in. Leave it in place for at least 30 seconds, remove it, clean it quickly (maybe on the tail) and read off the temperature. Dip it into some disinfectant, wipe it and return it to its case.

Pulse/heart rate this should be between about 35 to 45 beats per minute (bpm) in a resting pony. To take it, feel around where the main artery crosses the bone under the lower jaw just in front of the rounded part and leave your fingers in place, counting the pulses under them, for half a minute. Double it and you have the pulse rate, which is obviously the same as the heart rate.

Respiration stand behind and a little to one side of your pony and watch his opposite flank rise and fall, which can take a minute or so to spot, counting each rise-and-fall as one breath. It should be about 12 to 18 breaths per minute, maybe more in small ponies.

Dehydration this can be checked for by pressing your thumb firmly on the gum immediately above a corner front tooth to cause a pale patch. The colour should return within 1.5 seconds. Another check is to pinch up a fold of skin on the point of the shoulder, which should fall flat again immediately.

Gut sounds get used to listening to your pony's flanks to get an idea of his normal gut sounds. Absence of gut sounds, or excessive sounds, can indicate colic depending on its type.

Above: *Check your pony's body weight regularly. This pony looks in healthy condition, neither too fat nor too thin.*

Bodyweight

A big problem with native-type ponies and cobs is keeping their weight down, but it is a very common misconception that they do not need much feed. What they do need is the right *sort* of feed, and enough of it. As discussed earlier, energy levels should normally be kept down and you should aim to have only so much weight on your pony that you cannot see his ribs but can feel them quite easily. A little more weight (fat!) is allowed in grass-kept animals in winter.

Feet

The feet should be well shaped (see pages 67 and 94) with no cracks, undue chips, flaking horn or softened horn. The horn should be tough and resilient rather than hard and rigid and the hoof should have a natural sheen to it.

Teeth

The teeth are often out of sight and, therefore, out of mind. Have your pony's teeth checked every six months, more often if he is young or old, and watch his eating habits and movements carefully to check that he is not experiencing pain or discomfort.

Worms

Your vet (veterinarian) is the best person to advise you on whether or not your pony has a significant infestation of internal parasites or worms (they all have worms to some extent) and how to get rid of them.

Many owners 'worm' (give anti-worm drugs) haphazardly with no real idea of what they are doing. It is a good idea to take a couple of balls

condition scoring

This is a system of assessing your pony's condition using a scale of 0 to 5:

0 = emaciated
1 = **very thin**
2 = **lean**
3 = **correct condition**
4 = **fat**
5 = **obese**

It is a good plan to condition score your pony weekly.

of dung to your vet and ask to have a 'faecal count' done: this means counting under a microscope how many of what sort of worm eggs are present in the droppings, so that the vet can decide what drugs your pony should have, when and how often.

Different drugs are effective against different parasites and it is essential to give the right drug in the right amount at the right times of year and at the right intervals between doses.

All horses and ponies living together on a yard or field will have the same sort of infestation and should be wormed with the same drug at the same time, otherwise some worms will survive and breed drug-resistant offspring – and then you will have a problem getting rid of them.

TIP: *Worms can kill and can cause sickness and poor condition. Get rid of them.*

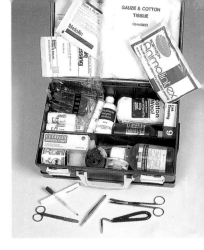

Above: *Keep a well-stocked, up-to-date first aid kit in your stable yard. Your vet is the best person to advise you about what should be included in it. Keep it clean and out of reach of young children.*

When should you call the vet (veterinarian)?

◆ You should arrange with your vet to perform a health check on your pony once a year, usually when he comes to give him his annual vaccinations and boosters. Your vet will devise a vaccination and worming programme for your pony and check his teeth, eyes and general health.

◆ Your vet will also be able to supply you with the best products for an up-to-date, comprehensive first-aid kit. Many products on the market are not the best things to use and your vet is the person who will have to sort out your pony when things go wrong, so take his or her advice.

◆ You should ring the vet when your pony does not show the signs of good health given above, when he has an injury you cannot deal with, when he is lame (limping, even slightly) or coughing or behaving abnormally.

◆ The veterinary practice will not mind at all your ringing to just discuss something: if it sounds as though a visit is needed they will probably say so. If you *know* a visit is needed, try to give plenty of notice for a non-urgent matter so that an appointment can be made, but if it is a real emergency tell them and they will get someone to you as soon as possible.

◆ You can also discuss your pony's health with other experienced people, particularly reliable professionals such as those who run your livery yard or riding school – but they are not substitutes for your vet. As they have a lot of experience, however, they may well be able to help you with a minor problem.

Wounds

These can look very frightening to a novice and should receive veterinary attention if more than one layer of skin is broken. Otherwise, you can deal with it yourself, with experienced help.

worm control

One very effective way of keeping infestation down is to remove droppings from paddocks and put them on the muck heap (do not pile them up in a corner of the field) at least every three days during the grazing season. Make this a strict routine, worm correctly and you will have very little trouble.

Below: *Ponies often rest a hind leg, like this, but note the fetlock on the right, which is badly swollen.*

Middle: *White socks usually mean that there is pink skin underneath them. These areas are very prone to mud fever, not only in winter. Keep a special eye on them because this disease will usually need veterinary treatment.*

Bottom: *Rain rash or rain scald is a disease similar to mud fever. It occurs on the neck, back and hindquarters, generally in warmer weather.*

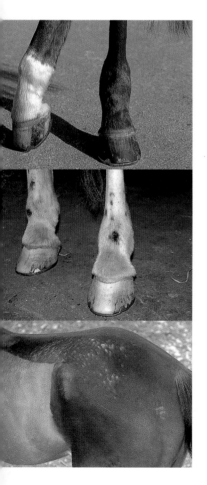

◆ Bathe wounds to clean them with cotton wool dipped in saline solution (about a level teaspoon of ordinary salt to 0.5l/1pt of clean, cold water).

◆ Put on a clean pad of lint or Gamgee Tissue over moistened, medicated gauze, and bandage carefully.

◆ Change the dressing daily.

TIP: *If a minor wound is not improving within a day or two, feels hot, discharges or is swollen, call the vet at once. For anything more serious, you should call the vet anyway.*

Signs of a sick pony

You should be concerned if:

◆ your pony looks miserable;

◆ has no energy;

◆ is keeping away from other ponies;

◆ has no interest in his surroundings;

◆ looks generally off-colour.

If this is the case, he could well be sick as opposed to just resting or sleeping. Take his temperature, pulse and respiration, get him into a well bedded-down stable, perhaps put a comfortable rug on him and call the vet. Learn from your veterinary book what to do whilst waiting for him or her to arrive, but do not hesitate to ring the surgery for instructions.

Ailments and illnesses

Colic

This is common in ponies fed incorrectly. It is a painful form of indigestion and can kill ponies so you always need to call the vet. The pony will be restless and uneasy, may paw the ground, look round at his sides anxiously, perhaps biting them, and may try to get down to roll in pain. If you spot any signs like this, ring the surgery for advice on what to do immediately and ask for a vet to come as soon as possible.

TIP: *Colicky ponies can become violent with pain so stay out of the stable if this happens, however concerned you are.*

Laminitis

This is a very painful foot disease most often caused by too much or unsuitable food. This disrupts the blood supply to the foot, and in really bad cases the foot can actually disintegrate and the pony has to be destroyed. The pony will be very reluctant to move, may not want to get up if down, may stand with his weight back on his heels (but not always) and may show patchy sweating. Do not force the pony to walk, remove all food and get the vet immediately.

Above: *This pony is too thin, as can be seen from his sunken back and prominent hip bones. He may not be getting enough nourishment from his paddock, or his teeth may need rasping or he may be infested with worms (internal parasites). He may even be suffering from all three conditions.*

Choke

Choke is a blockage of the gullet down which the food passes to the stomach (not of the windpipe). The pony may have discharges of saliva and undigested food from one or both nostrils, he will look very uncomfortable and keep trying to swallow. You may be able to gently feel or even see a lump on the underside of his neck. Call a vet at once.

Mud fever (legs) and rain rash/scald (back)

These occur when the skin is softened by over-exposure to wet and has been invaded by bacteria. The skin will be sore, warm and maybe swollen. The pony will be difficult to handle about the feet and legs and may be lame. The skin may be scabby and tufty in established cases, but you should notice that something is wrong before this happens. Neither of these conditions is a first-aid situation: you need veterinary attention. If the bacteria get into the bloodstream your pony may become very ill with blood poisoning.

There are *many* more conditions your pony can have, as you will see from your veterinary book, but the above are quite common and should be recognized.

Nursing

You may need to arrange a rota of people to look after a sick or injured pony if you do not keep him at a professional yard where the staff can be relied upon to nurse him properly. It is most important that this is done correctly so ignore people who tell you that there are more important things in life than your pony. That's only their opinion!

Get precise instructions from your vet about what to do, carry them out correctly, ring the surgery if you forget anything and get other help to handle your pony if necessary.

TIP: *NEVER FORGET: Owning any animal is a great responsibility and honour, and your pony is completely dependent on you for his care. Don't let him down.*

Index

Acknowledgements
All photography by
Kit Houghton